America's
DEADLIEST
TWISTER

The Tri-State Tornado of 1925

GEOFF PARTLOW

SOUTHERN ILLINOIS UNIVERSITY PRESS
CARBONDALE

Library of Congress Cataloging-in-Publication Data
Partlow, Geoff.
America's deadliest twister : the tri-state tornado of 1925 / Geoff Partlow.
    pages cm. — (Shawnee books)
Includes bibliographical references and index.
ISBN-13: 978-0-8093-3346-2 (pbk. : alk. paper)
ISBN-10: 0-8093-3346-5 (pbk. : alk. paper)
ISBN-13: 978-0-8093-3347-9 (ebook)
ISBN-10: 0-8093-3347-3 (ebook)
1. Tornadoes—Missouri—History—20th century. 2. Tornadoes—Illinois—His-
tory—20th century. 3. Tornadoes—Indiana—History—20th century. I. Title.
II. Title: Tri-state tornado of 1925.
QC955.5.U6P37 2014
551.55'3097709042—dc23   2013048223

AMERICA'S DEADLIEST TWISTER

 Shawnee Books

It is in the interest of mankind that there should be someone who is unconquerable, someone against whom fortune has no power.

—Seneca (4 BC–AD 65)

Contents

Illustrations

Acknowledgments

Writing is lonely business, an exercise in which one's companions are ideas and facts. The writer finds solace in the words themselves, words mined from one's mind to populate the page, orphans really, wide-eyed words that hope to find a home in the reader's heart.

"No man is an island," the poet John Donne said four hundred years ago, as true today as ever it was. Without the daily encouragement of my wife, Sarah, who nurtured me through so many crushing disappointments while I was trying to further my writing career, this would have indeed been a lonelier journey. Her support exceeds estimate.

And, too, a long list of friends, family, and loved ones who bolstered my all too fragile ego and passed out encouragement much like the folks who give water to runners in a marathon. Special mention goes to Jim and Mary Brigham, my amazing in-laws, whose enthusiasm is unbounded, and to my cuzzie Maria Partlow, who toughed it through opposing political stances to dish out attaboys when earned.

To Mike Greenwood, Duds, my friend, you cannot know how much your time given to reading and critiquing my stories has meant to me. I am thankful for your friendship. Stephanie Ryan, a helpful reader and, perhaps, toughest critic, has been generous with her time and interest, thank you. And Carolyn Boyles, an editor and writer friend in Arkansas who reaches back forty years in my life and who shares my passion for words. Your expertise and guidance have been invaluable.

Thanks go out to the many librarians who helped find research for the story. Yes, I know you were just doing your jobs, but many of you went way, way beyond mere duty. The Benton Public Library, West Frankfort Public Library, and Carbondale Public Library were most helpful, as was the Sally Logan Library in Murphysboro and the Brehm Library in Mt. Vernon. Microfilm archives at the Delyte W. Morris Library on the campus of Southern Illinois University Carbondale and the Olin Library at Washington University in St. Louis offered treasure troves of information held within their newspaper database. Thank you, Jackson County Historical Society of Illinois. And a special thank-you to Jim Jones at the West Franklin Historical District and Silkwood Inn Museum. Jim's thorough perusal of the society's digital archives and generous sharing of those images were incredibly helpful. And thank you, Mary Ellen and Winona, the wonderful caretakers and archivists at the Frankfort Area Historical Museum. Lecta and Diane at the White County Historical Society welcomed me to their Carnegie Library and opened up everything they had on the Tri-State Tornado, as did Anna Shelton at the Hamilton County Historical Society in the historic and beautiful McCoy Library, both organizations giving top-drawer service with plenty of friendly smiles to go with it.

A heartfelt thank-you goes out to Karl Kageff and his brilliant staff at Southern Illinois University Press, whose professional, collective expertise helped hone my first attempt at writing nonfiction into a book far more readable and accurate than I could ever hope to produce alone. You made my dream come true, and for that, I am grateful.

AMERICA'S DEADLIEST TWISTER

1

Genesis, 1 P.M.:
Annapolis, Missouri, to Gorham, Illinois

The official National Weather Bureau forecast for Wednesday, March 18, 1925, issued for the southern reaches of Missouri, Illinois, and Indiana called for "rains and strong shifting winds," a prediction that was a tragedy of understatement. The tempest that formed in the Missouri Ozarks that afternoon became the most lethal tornado in the history of the United States and the third deadliest in the recorded history of the world, forever altering the economy of southern Illinois.

With Easter just three weeks away, the Tri-State Tornado dropped from the sky during the era of the Charleston, flappers, Charles Lindbergh, and Prohibition. Calvin Coolidge of Plymouth Notch, Vermont, was president, and the Ku Klux Klan was at peak membership. That year, Adolf Hitler published *Mein Kampf*, blue-eyed Paul Newman was born, and Chrysler Corporation was founded. In small-town Dayton, Tennessee, William Jennings Bryan and Clarence Darrow squabbled over evolution in the Scopes Trial. Bryan was born in Salem, a central Illinois city that would later send troops to help the dispossessed.

Spring training that day saw the St. Louis Browns whip the Brooklyn Dodgers 3-0, and the Cardinals, under the immortal Branch Rickey, with the franchise on the cusp of its forty-fourth season in St. Louis, lost to the Oakland (California) Oaks of the Pacific Coast League. That season the Cardinals' player-manager, Rogers Hornsby, hit .403, belted 39 home runs, and delivered 143 RBIs. The stats earned Hornsby the National League Most Valuable Player Award.

This, too, was the era when ubiquitous local newspapers carried endearingly folksy sections like "The Talk of the Walk," "Our Neighborhood," or "All around the Town," the latter being the case in the *Daily Independent* in Murphysboro, Illinois, a town squarely in the crosshairs of the tornado. Usually found in the interior pages of an edition, the columns chronicle the comings and goings of townspeople. The day of the tornado, it was reported in Murphysboro that "Attorney. L. R. Stewart went to St. Louis on business Wednesday morning. . . . Reverend Marion Wilson of Pinckneyville passed through the city Tuesday enroute to Willisville where he is holding a revival meeting."

Such was the quiet world in the path of a historic storm that no one had any inkling was on the way. Children went off to schools that morning whose administrations were unprepared for the tragedy about to occur. Fathers and brothers traveled to work in the coal mines, farms, and stores of the region. A long winter had given way to the dangerous gift of the first warm day of the year. In Murphysboro, DeSoto, and West Frankfort, some of the very people mentioned in "The Talk of the Walk" and columns like it throughout the region would not live to read about their neighbors again.

Before the sun set, 695 people were to die.

D. W. Griffith's silent screen classic *Birth of a Nation*, based on Thomas Dixon's best-selling novel *The Clansman,* was released in 1915. A classmate and social friend of Dixon at Johns Hopkins University, Virginia-born President Woodrow Wilson quipped after a private showing in the White House that the movie was "like writing history with lightning." The movie rekindled the horror that was the Ku Klux Klan. A decade after its first release, *Birth of a Nation* was still playing at the Barth Theatre in Carbondale, Illinois, a business owned by I. W. Rogers and his Gem Theatre Company of Cairo. Adults got in for forty cents, children fifteen. The quarter-page advertisement in the *Free Press* that Wednesday called the movie "a story of epic proportion, not to be missed," but few events can compare before or since to the epic that was on its way from the Missouri Ozarks.

On that early spring day, southeast Missouri and the southern-most parts of Illinois and Indiana were awash in welcome warmth. In Carbondale, a proximate town to DeSoto and Murphysboro, the high temperature was 69°F. The *Alton Evening Telegraph* the day after the storm said, "A violent snowstorm fringed the tornado on the north when it struck Wednesday. [The] Weather Bureau predicts freezing or [slightly] above in the devastated region tonight." The bureau was right about the cold but woefully inaccurate in predicting the possibility of tornadoes. Indeed, survivors did report snow flurries in West Frankfort, Illinois, the evening of the storm.

During the morning of the gathering storm, a deep, deep low-pressure area sucked balmy and moist air chock-full of energy from the Gulf of Mexico. At the same time, a high-pressure Canadian cold front clippered south on a collision course. The weather extremes battled one another for dominance. A war between winter and spring, north and south was about to be engaged in deadly fashion, a war no one was going to win.

First spotted by a mail carrier in his horse and buggy at approximately 1:00 P.M., the vortex formed and touched down in rural Ozarks upcountry north-northwest of Ellington, Missouri. Once in contact with the ground, it began tracking northeast on a relentless course of sixty-nine degrees across the forested hills at seventy-two miles per hour, an unmatched US record for a tornado's forward land speed. The storm averaged an astonishing sixty-two miles an hour through its life.

At first, the Tri-State was no more than a fitful F2 category storm, a ghostly gray sinuous rope spinning along. then pulling up into the dark clouds several times until the vortex finally landed for good. It then caused utter destruction for the next three and a half hours on a continuous track of 219 miles through three states and thirteen counties. No recorded storm had done that before, nor has it happened since.

Colored by debris and dirt pulled into the vortex, the powerful funnel changed from gray to black. Once the vortex reached rich farmlands along the Mississippi River, wind velocity ramped to make it an F5 on the Fujita scale of tornado strength. Wind speeds exceeded three hundred miles per hour, but forward speed declined to sixty-two miles per hour. The tornado averaged a half mile in width, but at times, engorged with debris, it exceeded a mile across; some even reported three miles, but that assertion is likely folklore.

Survivors recounted stories of being trapped inside houses launched off their foundations to rotate in kinship with the winds in scenes identical to Dorothy's house at the opening to the *Wizard of Oz*. Others told stories of witnessing houses and barns lifted into the roiled air only to be dropped hundreds of yards away, the structures reduced to haphazard piles of kindling. Whole towns were swept clean to look like the barren and bloody battlefields of France in World War I, while fires from displaced cookstoves and kerosene lamps ignited rubble, incinerating victims ensnared under debris, horrifying would-be rescuers who could only listen helplessly to the dying's tortured screams.

THE FUJITA SCALE OF TORNADO STRENGTH

F	Wind Speeds (mph)	Characteristic Damage
0	40–72	Light damage—signage blown down, small trees uprooted, chimneys toppled, tree branches on the ground
1	73–112	Moderate damage—outbuildings destroyed, shingles peeled, mobile homes pushed off foundations, vehicles blown from roadways
2	113–157	Extensive damage—large trees snapped off, entire roofs torn from buildings, mobile homes twisted apart, vehicles overturned but not moved
3	158–206	Severe damage—vehicles pushed or rolled along the ground, roofs completely ripped off, walls collapsed, pavement possibly blown away
4	207–260	Devastating damage—bark stripped from trees, well-made houses demolished, vehicles borne considerable distances and smashed, forest trees down and aligned on the ground
5	261–318	Utter destruction—empty foundations a key feature; home sites cleared of debris; supernatural event phenomena (e.g., straw embedded in boards); people, animals, autos, farm machinery, and trucks carried aloft

SOURCES: Adapted from Wallace Akin, *The Forgotten Storm: The Great Tri-State Tornado of 1925* (Guilford, CT: Lyons, 2002), xiv–xv, and Peter S. Felknor, *The Tri-State Tornado: The Story of America's Greatest Tornado Disaster* (Ames: Iowa State University Press, 1992), appendix B.

After the twister flattened 90 percent of the buildings in Annapolis, Missouri, killing four and injuring twenty-five and leaving a thousand people homeless, it gave the same treatment to Leadanna, a company town the St. James Lead Mining Corporation owned, where two more people died. The least-damaged building in Annapolis, 111 miles south of St. Louis, was the school, a rare piece of good news along the seventy-mile Missouri track, not to be repeated that afternoon.

The tornado traversed the red oak–encrusted hills of the Ozarks through numerous upland Missouri farms. It was here, rotating through the little towns of Lixville, Schumer Springs, and Frohna with an aggregate

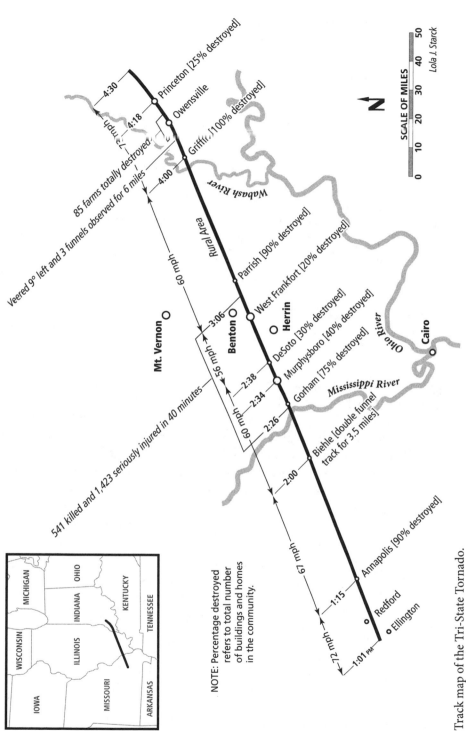

Track map of the Tri-State Tornado.
Adapted from John W. Wilson and Stanley A. Changnon Jr., Illinois Tornadoes, circular 103 (Urbana: Illinois State Water Survey, 1971), 33.

Lola J. Starck

SCALE OF MILES
0   10   20   30   40   50

N

Princeton [25% destroyed]
4:30
Owensville
4:18
85 farms totally destroyed
Veered 9° left and 3 funnels observed for 6 miles
Griffin [100% destroyed]
4:00
Wabash River

Rural Area

Parrish [90% destroyed]
West Frankfort [20% destroyed]
60 mph
Mt. Vernon
3:06
Benton
Herrin
DeSoto [30% destroyed]
56 mph
Murphysboro [40% destroyed]
2:38
60 mph
2:34
Gorham [75% destroyed]
Ohio River
Cairo
2:26
541 killed and 1,423 seriously injured in 40 minutes
Biehle [double funnel track for 3.5 miles]
Mississippi River
2:00
Annapolis [90% destroyed]
67 mph
1:15
Redford
Ellington
72 mph
1:01 PM

NOTE: Percentage destroyed
refers to total number
of buildings and homes
in the community.

WISCONSIN   MICHIGAN
IOWA   ILLINOIS   INDIANA   OHIO
MISSOURI   KENTUCKY
ARKANSAS   TENNESSEE

population of a hundred souls, that the tornado morphed into a dangerous double vortex that killed ten more, finishing off the small town of Biehle before entering the fertile Mississippi River valley. Five schoolchildren died in little Lixville. Ten percent of Missourians unlucky enough to be in the tornado's path died.

About 2:25 P.M., according to Fountain Bluff Township supervisor Julius Moeckel, "[t]he storm crossed the Mississippi River into Illinois at Big Lake Ditch where lived the ferryman, Martin Miesner. His home was built on the original sturdy log house from early days when this was the Illinois Territory. Everything went but the logs. Miesner and his family were saved by the log walls."[1]

The tornado crossed over the Mississippi River to enter an area known to locals as Egypt. It was this destination beginning in the early nineteenth century that emigrants risked their lives and those of their families for a new beginning away from the plantation culture of the old south. Egypt offered raw opportunity and a chance to own large tracts of land; both achievements impossibilities in the states from which these families fled. Theirs was a classic odyssey for freedom that of necessity bred a fiercely independent people.

On the spring-softened afternoon, the innocent and oblivious inhabitants of Gorham, Illinois, were unaware of their mortal danger. In mere seconds, thirty-four people died violent deaths.[2] Of the eighty houses in the five-hundred-population town, only twenty were left standing, every one of them suffering degrees of damage so severe they were uninhabitable.

A farming town in the heart of the American Bottom surrounded by some of the most fertile agricultural property in the world, Gorham served a heritage extending back nine thousand years when Native Americans arrived after the Illinoian glacier gradually receded to the Arctic. Glacial melt waters scoured the American Bottom from sandstone and limestone bluffs and birthed the Mississippi River to run its course in between the very bluffs the water wore into existence. Crops, particularly corn, flourished in the deep alluvial topsoil of the flood plain. Native Americans also created petroglyphs pecked into the bluffs close to Gorham, many with a cross in circle or a swastika enclosed; both images' religious shorthand representing the cosmos of the Native Americans' Mississippian culture.

Late in the seventeenth century, the French recognized the value of the area. They began to develop the Bottoms and would live and love there until they lost the French and Indian War to the British in 1765. Most but not all French habitants moved across the river to establish such future cities in Missouri as St. Louis and Cape Girardeau and the towns of New

Madrid and Ste. Genevieve, but some French stayed and are ancestors to the Gorham residents of 1925.

One wonders if over the millennia residents ever saw the match of the storm that crossed the river unwaveringly tracking to Gorham just three miles inland.

Clocks in Gorham homes stopped at 2:25 P.M.

The town doctor was seeing patients in his home office, giving two of them inoculations. Both patients died instantly. Only the doctor's collarbone was broken.

Judith Cox was bored that Wednesday afternoon. Like many families in town whose men worked for the Missouri Pacific Railroad, her railroad foreman husband was away for the day. She had just fed her two teenaged children lunch. The Gorham School was close; in fact, everything was close in the town. Judith worried about the unsettled weather, worried that the kids were going to be soaked by one of the frequent showers that were off and on all morning, but luck was on the Cox family's side at least for now.

Her children safely back at school, Judith decided she could use a coffee down to Wallace's, Gorham's only restaurant, and some companionship as well. She donned a raincoat with her husband's paycheck in the side pocket, thinking she would deposit it in the First National Bank of Gorham with nice Ernie Swartz after she had a cup of coffee and maybe some of Katie White's famous chess pie.

Judith sat down with her friend Lulu Moschenrose, settling into a pleasant, free-range tittle-tattle decidedly better than ironing, the very task Judith was avoiding. Outside grew darker and darker as though a giant had positioned itself between the sun and Gorham, and then Gorham went silent. Not a puff of wind stirred. Thunder rumbled ominously to the west. Birds no longer sang. The horizon was lined with verdigris clouds lit by yellow lightning. Familiar with signs pointing to a hard storm, Judith became greatly alarmed. She jumped to her feet, excused herself from Lulu, and told her friend she was going to run to the school just in the other block to fetch her children before the storm hit. And then the wall cloud smashed Wallace's.

"I opened the door, bent my head down against the wind," she recounted to a *St. Louis Post Dispatch* reporter. The force stripped the raincoat from her body and threw her back into the restaurant where she ended up jammed against the hot coal stove. "The whole building seemed to shiver. It rocked back and forth. There was groaning and creaking. Fire was flashing in great puffs from the stove. I had to get away from it. I was afraid I would be burned to death. Then the walls fell in. The roof was falling. Something hit me on the head. I came to under boards and timbers. Near me was a red cow which seemed to sort of take the weight off me."

Joe Moschenrose, a butcher and Lulu's brother, ran into what was left of Wallace's. Chunks of ridiculously large hail covered the ruins, and it was pouring down cold rain. He spotted Judith and lifted boards from her and the cow as well. Like something from a Marc Chagall print, the red cow rose on unsteady feet and tottered off.

Alive and chatting about life just moments before, "[t]here on the floor with a great gash on her head was Lulu. She was dead. Joe and I went to [what was left of] the kitchen. I helped him search the debris. Together we dug out . . . Katie White. She was dead, horribly crushed." In the end, Joe learned he was the only Moschenrose left. Four of his family died that afternoon: Mrs. Mary, Louise (Lulu), Edward, and Andrew.

In a panic, Judith scurried toward Gorham School. Inexplicably, the raincoat stripped from her had sailed up in a tree within easy reach. The paycheck was still in the pocket. Pieces of houses, chairs, clothing, boots, a Singer sewing machine—the detritus of what had been life in Gorham was strewn in her path. The school grounds were a chaos of crying children, some screaming in pain. Boards that had been roof rafters were piled all around the front of the three-story brick edifice. "Mothers and fathers were silently weeping," she said, and she was greatly relieved to find her children relatively unscathed. "Thank God they are still alive," she told the *St. Louis Post-Dispatch*. Her children's faces were peppered with "splinters and sand that had been blown with such force it was embedded in their skin."[3]

Total destruction along the Missouri Pacific Railroad tracks in Gorham, Illinois. *Photo courtesy of the Jackson County Historical Society of Illinois.*

Among Judith Cox's neighbors was the Temure family, who lived on the edge of town. Before the storm hit, seventy-year-old Alice Temure, who was partially paralyzed by what was thought to have been a stroke, lay in bed. Her son, Paul, the village blacksmith, was in the next room, and husband, George, was standing outside the window, watching the worsening weather. "It grew dark," Alice told the *Post-Dispatch*. "Rain poured down then the wind struck. The house lifted in the air must have been ten feet and we was whirled right around on the big elm in the backyard. The branches, they stuck through the windows. Then they was a great splintering and cracking and the wall fell out."

Alice remembered nothing more until she regained consciousness. She was lying in the mud of a fallow cornfield up and over a hill behind the house. Her immoveable feet came to rest in a creek. "At my side was my husband. A great spike had been driven through his [hip]," she told the reporter. "'I'm dying, Alice, dear,' [George] groaned to her. And we laid there and prayed together."

Paul finally found them. He scooped his injured father in his arms to carry him back to the shattered remnants of what was once their home, now hanging in an elm tree. Paul made his father as comfortable as possible and then fetched Alice. By the time they returned, George was dead.[4]

In times of trouble, "makeshift" becomes the watchword. Such was the case in Gorham. The basement of the leveled school was pressed into service as a temporary morgue. At least, the nearly intact first floor offered a token roof over the dead. The Missouri Pacific Railroad took most of the Gorham injured to hospitals in East St. Louis, but some were delivered to Dupo, Illinois, just south of St. Louis, and to St. Mary's Hospital in Cairo, Illinois.

Witnesses described a tornado three-quarters of a mile wide but not formed like a normal funnel cloud; rather, it was a dark, churning fog with gray wisps of siphoned Mississippi River water whipped to froth. Eighteen Missouri Pacific boxcars were blown over by this cloud, rendered unusable, and the train depot was obliterated. Every storefront in town was blown out. Gorham was gone.

"Ernest Swartz, Cashier of the First National Bank," the *Benton (IL) Evening News* reported on March 21,

> heard the approach of the tornado, grabbed the money and records and rushed into the vault. Just as he closed the door the building caved in. Only one $20 bill was lost. Swartz said that after the storm he picked up all the silver money he had been unable to clutch in his dash to safety. The day previous, Swartz had talked about a storm

with his mother, and told her that he would follow the course he did if one should approach. She warned him not to go into the vault, because of the possibility of his being killed by a poison gas protection device. Today she said she was "tickled pink" because her son disregarded her advice.

Not so fortunate were eleven lifelong friends gathered on a blustery day to play cards in the repair bay of one of the town's few filling stations. All eleven died.[5]

Fire was not an issue in Gorham although one house did burn with three people trapped, but the victims were presumed dead before the flames consumed the house remnants.

Food, as well as drinking water, quickly became a problem, one alleviated by a Red Cross relief train from St. Louis that reached Gorham in the early evening.

The *Murphysboro Independent* in a March 23 front-page story said with obvious appreciation, "Makanda and Grand Tower . . . along with Cobden took Gorham to heart and cared for them. Ed Becker closed his box factory [which had made boxwood boxes for the area's thriving fruit industry], and Charlie McCann called on his bully-boys from the quarry and construction camp and you should have seen them clean up Gorham, more than two hundred of them."

By May, the rebuilding of Gorham was in full swing. Brigadier General Carlos E. Black of the Illinois National Guard and assistant quartermaster in charge of the relief supply depot in Carbondale, toured the area on May 8. In a report sent to Isaac (Ike) Levy, chairman of the Murphysboro Relief Committee, Black wrote, "[In] Gorham I found 50 families living in tents. Twenty of the 50 families have already started to rebuild their homes."[6]

2

▼

Murphysboro, Illinois

Hugging the course of the Big Muddy River, the storm advanced toward Murphysboro, a busy city of thirteen thousand, a rail and manufacturing center at the time, and the Jackson County seat, which it is today. The tornado crossed the river on the city's southwest outskirts at Buster Brown Park, named for the Brown Shoe Company's most popular shoe of the day and made in that town.

Brown Shoe Company plant No. 7, Murphysboro, Illinois, postcard postmarked 1917. A coal-fired steam power plant, replete with smokestack and water tower, is on the right. *From the author's collection.*

Brown Shoe's plant No. 7, the Murphysboro factory, opened in 1910, and in 1923, its employees made twenty-two thousand pairs of shoes a week. A St. Louis corporation founded in 1878, Brown Shoe was listed on the New York Stock Exchange in 1913 under the ticker symbol BWS, the Murphysboro *Daily Independent* reported on October 16, 1923. At the time of the tornado, five hundred "Brownies" worked in a building whose top two stories were gone when the storm was over. Brown Shoe was quick to rebuild.

Another industry hit by the tornado, Murphysboro Paving Brick Company, begun in 1902 by Henry H. Jenkins and William H. Hill, made paving bricks under the brand name "Egyptian." A thriving manufacturing entity as well as a contract paving company with global scope, the company at its peak employed 125 men, fired twenty-one kilns with good southern Illinois coal, used locally mined clay shale, and produced as many as eighty thousand pavers a day. The twenty-five-acre brickyard made as many as eleven million bricks a year. All three local railroads, the Mobile and Ohio (M&O), the Illinois Central (IC), and the Missouri Pacific, maintained spurs to the plant, giving the company distribution channels to meet market demand nationwide. Under contract from its bustling center north of the city, the

Murphysboro Paving Brick Company yard, ca. 1920. Kilns are on the left, finished bricks are stacked four high on the ground and in higher stacks to the right. M&O railcars await loading. *Photo courtesy of the Jackson County Historical Society of Illinois.*

plant shipped five million bricks to help build the infrastructure of the Panama Canal between 1904 and 1914, stated the October 16, 1923, *Murphysboro Daily Independent*. Many of Murphysboro's finest homes were constructed or reconstructed after the tornado with Egyptian-brand building bricks, and, of course, the company had a monopoly with the city's streets. Many city streets in Egypt are still paved by the attractive red bricks.

Four days after the storm, the company's secretary, F. F. Robison, who had purchased Jenkins's shares in 1917, promised, "We will resume manufacturing at once when electric power is restored. The storm did not touch our plant. We are assured power within a few days."[1] The business closed in the early 1930s, a victim of the Great Depression and the emergence of "hard roads," southern Illinois vernacular for paved roads, to carry auto and truck traffic.

Another employer was Reliance Milling Company, officially started up in 1877 as the Dean Milling Company and owned and run by the Dean family of Ava, Illinois. The mill daily produced thirty barrels, about three tons, of flour and was a successor of several operations dating to the Civil War, an era when farmers drove to Murphysboro in horse- or mule-drawn wagons, the back filled with kids and burlap sacks of corn and wheat to be custom ground. On October 16, 1923, the *Daily Independent* in Murphysboro reported that a fire razed the facility in 1894, and the mill was rebuilt the following year. Ed Sauer bought the business in 1904, changed the name to Reliance Milling, remodeled it three years later, and increased daily capacity to as much as five hundred barrels. The Dean family bought it back in 1912. "The local properties are equipped with the latest improved machinery," the 1923 *Daily Independent* article crowed, "and the quality of its products second to none. The Reliance and the Ava properties have a combined capacity of 1,000 barrels per day. Leading brands manufactured here are American Lady, their highest grade flour, Paragon Self-Rising, and New Moon hard wheat flour. These brands have long been a great favorite in the Southland where they are as well-known as they are in the city where they are made." The Dean family decided not to rebuild.

Also damaged was the processing plant of Isco-Bautz Silica and Feldspar Company, with Illinois offices at 1808 Walnut Street. Raw minerals that the company mined from the American Bottom bluffs at Wolf Lake, near Gorham, were lugged by both the IC and the Missouri Pacific to Isco-Bautz's Murphysboro operation east of the Big Muddy River where the ore was refined into superior-grade silica marketed to glass manufacturers, high-grade paper companies, and fine china kilns throughout the United States. Management rebuilt the heavily damaged engine house after the storm and resumed production.

Reliance mill before the tornado. *From a contemporary penny postcard.*

Reliance mill after the tornado. *From a contemporary penny postcard.*

THE RAILROADS

The importance of railroads to the regional economy as well as their role in facilitating the recovery of the overwhelmed area cannot be overstated. The M&O rail yards in Murphysboro employed about fourteen hundred, making it the largest employer in the city. Assuming that the typical family had four members, nearly half of the city's population was sustained by M&O. When employees of other railroads serving the area are added, the relative importance of the railroad industry grows even larger. For southern Illinois, Murphysboro was the rule rather than the exception.

The IC and M&O maintained thriving operations in Murphysboro. In 1897 the IC bought what was the oldest railroad in Illinois, the Mount Carbon Coal Company of Murphysboro, chartered in 1835 to ship coal mined from the area to the Mississippi River port of Grand Tower, eighteen miles southwest. The name was changed on April 6, 1869, to the Grand Tower Manufacturing and Transportation Railroad. This railroad was linked with the Carbondale and Shawneetown Line with the intention to connect the Ohio River at Shawneetown to the bustling Mississippi River port of Grand Tower.

One of the south's premier railroads prior to the Civil War and the region's second land-grant build-out, M&O was headquartered in Mobile,

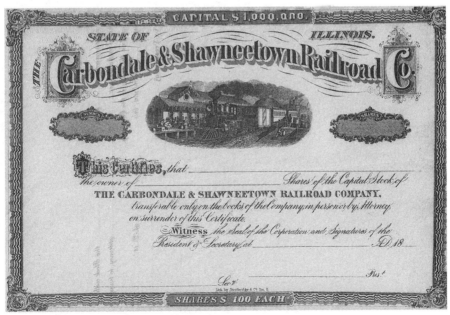

Carbondale and Shawneetown Railroad uncirculated stock certificate, ca. 1871. The vignette is a fine engraving of what a post–Civil War depot might have looked like. *From the author's collection.*

Alabama. It figured prominently in the Civil War but was virtually destroyed during the hostilities. The company threatened bankruptcy after Appomattox but survived to buy the narrow-gauge St. Louis and Cairo Railroad, which chugged through Murphysboro, on May 1, 1882.

The Missouri Pacific Railroad served the area, too. Originally organized by New York financier Jay Gould, upon his death in 1892, the major east-west railroad passed from the extensive estate to his son George, who ran it into bankruptcy. Up from the ashes following a merger with the St. Louis, Iron Mountain, and Southern Railway, the Missouri Pacific was operating again under new ownership.

Trains provided passenger service, coal transportation, merchandise delivery from urban wholesalers, mail-order distribution from Sears Roebuck and Montgomery Ward, and shipment of fruits and vegetables grown in southwestern Illinois, particularly apples, strawberries, and peaches from the Illinois Ozarks around Cobden, Anna, and Alto Pass. Measured by tonnage, in the latter part of the nineteenth century in Egypt, commercial merchandise was the leading freight, followed by coal, then corn, then lumber.

Labor-intensive steam-locomotive repair facilities existed in Murphysboro and Carbondale. Beginning in the first few years of the 1900s, the era's mass transit was interurban trolley roads that ran regular schedules from Murphysboro to Carterville, Herrin, and Marion in Williamson County. Many a southern Illinois coal miner rode to work on an interurban car. The Murphysboro Electric Railway and Light Company laid three miles of track within the city but later expanded the road seven miles east to the university town of Carbondale. By 1927, most of the trolleys were supplanted by more modern automobiles or bus lines.[2]

THE TOLL ON THE PEOPLE

A mile-wide Tri-State Tornado traveled the six miles from Gorham to Murphysboro in as many minutes, arriving at the southwest edge of the city at 2:34 P.M. Nearly 40 percent of the county seat was destroyed. The Murphysboro death toll was 234, a figure that remains a record total for an American town's loss. Nearly 1,000 people were injured. Twenty-five of the dead were children killed while school was in session, which is the second-highest tornado-related school death toll in the nation's history.

The pathos of so many deaths in such a relatively small town must have been unbearable. People knew one another and cared. One paid attention to a siren in the night because one would likely know who was going to the emergency room or who was going to jail.

This story of a man found dead in the ruins of the M&O yards is a fitting example. "Last Wednesday's cyclone violated the heart secret of Louis J. Gualdoni and his bride, Miss Gladys L. Harrell," married on January 23 in Desoto, Missouri, the *Murphysboro Daily Independent* related on March 23, 1925. "[The couple] jealously guarded their secret intending to have the edge on friends who had meant to chivari them here. Just another heart story, but one hard to tell."[3] The same paper also lists Louis Gualdoni in a death notice: twenty-six years, seven months, and one day old, the son of John living on Route 7, and a machinist apprentice. Gladys Harrell's name does not appear in the long list of Murphysboro's dead or injured.

Another M&O employee, "Buster" Brown, was last seen at the water cooler. "No trace of 'Buster' has been found."[4]

Murphysboro's leveled residential areas, totaling twelve hundred buildings, would not be completely repaired or repopulated until the end of World War II, two decades later.

The tornado twisted out of usefulness machines of steel bolted to the floor and flattened the M&O Railroad locomotive repair yard, roundhouse, and car manufacturing center, one block east of Longfellow grade school. Of the five hundred workers on duty that day, thirty-five died, most of whom burned to death. Two hundred employees had to be carried to hospitals. One worker saved his life by crawling into the cold firebox of a locomotive under repair. Another found refuge in the maintenance pit underneath an engine.

M&O rail shops before the tornado, ca. 1915. *From the author's collection.*

Man walking the wreckage of the M&O rail yards in Murphysboro. A locomotive stands in the center of the image near reserve wheels and axles while the ruins still smolder. *From a contemporary postcard.*

A man was buried for two days as firemen and volunteers tried to dig him out only to lose him, his cries of agony wrenching their hearts when the fires finally consumed him.

"My grandfather, he worked for the railroad, the one on the west end of town," ninety-three-year-old Eileen Breeden Jones said to the author in her tidy living room as she relaxed in a lavender plush chair, her accustomed place to watch TV and stitch intricate quilt squares. Eileen was seven years old in 1925.

> He worked underneath the [steam] engines in that big pit, and they put those engines on there, and I guess he greased 'em or oiled 'em or whatnot, and they told him, "It's gonna storm, you better come on up and outta there." And he said, "If it's gonna be a bad one, I'm better off down here than up there," and so that's where he was down there in that pit. Saved his life, 'cause that end of town was hit bad. All I remember is all the chaos and stuff goin' on, ya know. There was a lot of smoke.

Eileen's right hand cut through the air, describing the scene. For a moment she looked away from the author but right into her memory. "You can't imagine. Course, now our end of town wasn't hit that bad, I mean they had damages to their roofs and things. But the fires were comin', and I was scared, what with a change of clothes under my arm in case . . . well, ya know . . . in case."[5]

S. R. Stannard, a reporter for the *St. Louis Post-Dispatch*, related a story told by an M&O foreman of an African American workman in the yards who was helping with rescue efforts when he found the decapitated body of his brother; "He kept on working in an effort to save fellow workmen who were in danger of being burned to death before they could be reached."

In the same evening edition of March 21, Stannard told of an interview with a Carbondale fireman two days after the tornado in which the fireman said the rail yard was still smoldering: "The screams of a man being burned to death were heard from the ruins, but he was buried so deeply [nobody] could . . . reach him [in time]."

The M&O lost thirteen steam engines undergoing repair. Each engine cost $25,000 to replace. Most reports estimated the railroad's total loss at $1.5 million ($19.4 million today).[6]

In a 1992 interview, Murphysboro native Eugene Porter said his "father was on a switch engine, switching south of town, and when they saw the storm, they just cut out because they knew it was a bad one. He was at a brewery that was still making beer, even though it was illegal in '25, and they was switching beer out of there. Anyway, the train blew off." The switch engine "derailed. It was that much of a storm," concluded Porter.[7]

The Rudolph Stecher Brewing Company, the only such business of its kind in Murphysboro at the time of the tornado, produced forty thousand barrels of beer a year, employed eighty men, and boasted a capitalization of $800,000 by 1910.[8] During Prohibition, Stecher Brewing produced near beer legally in accordance with the statutes of 1919's Volstead Act, which allowed beverages with 0.5 percent alcohol or less. Legal records show that the company was taken to court several times during Prohibition for allegedly brewing the real thing, as Porter suggested in his interview.

Logan and Longfellow grade schools and Murphysboro High School were heavily damaged. When the city's survivors learned of the destruction, they raced to assist. In the *Murphysboro Daily Independent*'s first publication after the storm, its editor describes his personal account in breathless prose:

Someone shouted [in the streets], "The school fell on the children, the Logan School."

A race through clogged alleys and streets, then across to Fourteenth [Street], and came into view a stream of school children

The Rudolph Stecher brewery, 1320 Rover Street, Murphysboro, about 1907. M&O railcars are parked on the siding. *From a contemporary penny postcard.*

running from the terror, then the old Logan School wreckage. A few men and several frantic mothers looking for their children. The numbers grew. The east half down stairs had held up the wreckage from above and most of the pupils there got out, many bleeding. Up the brick pile on the south some more men were digging children from under the brick on the second story floor. Most of them at the start were able to climb down assisted by two men each, a few had to be carried. Then a dead pupil, two, three, four. Police Chief, Joe Boston, found his little daughter, dead.

She was Evelyn, eight years old.

In 1992 Murphysboro resident Wilma Theiss Kimmel furnished a moving description of the aftershock of the Tri-State Tornado: "My brother Jack was a 6th grade pupil at Logan school, two blocks away on 15th Street, where we attended school, including Mama in the 1890s. After we ate lunch, Papa [home from his railroad engineer's job for dinner] showed us fruit he had bought that morning. . . . We were allowed a sampling before we went our separate ways."[9]

Her father stayed under the shade tree in the backyard to get the fruit ready for canning. Wilma went back for afternoon classes at Murphysboro

Township High School, her mother returned to work at Brown Shoe, and Jack to Logan School, which the school board had recently voted to replace due to its unsafe construction of sun-dried, soft brick.

The tornado passed. Wilma left school and carefully walked through live electric lines toward home, on the way finding her mother, who sent her to find Jack and her father.

I began to run when I saw the school a crumpled pile of bricks at the same time I saw a small figure standing in the middle of what I thought was the street, waving and screaming.

Someone had put on him a long, oversize coat that hung a foot beyond his hands and fell to the ground. I didn't know whether to laugh or cry, when I recognized Jack. . . . He told me he crawled out of the 2nd story window when the walls collapsed in the schoolroom. . . . I found him not knowing what to do, where to go, or what had happened.

On March 18, [Jack] calls every year. When I answer the phone, he says, "Hullo! Do you know what day this is?" I tease, and answer, "No, what day is it?" We laugh together, then we remember one more time, and we don't laugh.[10]

Logan School ruins. The oldest school building in the city, it was constructed of sun-dried bricks. *Photo courtesy of the Jackson County Historical Society of Illinois.*

J. E. Fischer, principal of Longfellow School, was burrowing in the debris right along with many other men, some frantic parents, some just volunteers anxiously looking for two missing first-graders. "There was a terrific roar," Fischer said of the harrowing experience when the tornado smacked the school. "The building began to rumble," and he ran into the central hallway of the u-shaped three-story schoolhouse, where he had ordered the 450 children to assemble, his thinking being that an interior, windowless hallway would offer shelter. But the building was beginning to disintegrate. Fischer was confronted with a life-or-death problem: remain inside a structure that threatened to come down on their heads or risk running outside into the teeth of the storm with lethal debris whipping across the schoolyard. Yelling above the roar of the wind, he instructed the school's ten teachers to escort students out the door. "I suppose half of them were outside when the tornado struck in its full fury," he said. "The building crumbled and came down in a terrible heap around the heads of the children trapped inside."[11] Ten innocents died from their injuries, yet that number, as tragic as it is, would likely have been far worse had Fischer been less proactive.

Murphysboro schools reopened Monday, March 30, with the generous help of the Lions Club International. Through local chapters, the organization contributed $10,000 worth of supplies and textbooks to all districts the storm impacted. High school students reported to the patched-up township facility on Spruce Street. Children who had attended Logan or Longfellow Schools were taught in church basements throughout the city.

Remains of Longfellow School. The surrounding area has been swept clean by the winds. *From a contemporary postcard.*

Damaged high school. The city of Murphysboro had just completed a $267,000 addition to the campus. *From a contemporary postcard.*

Michael Kiley was an engineer for an M&O passenger train. Throttling down his powerful steam locomotive as it crossed the Big Muddy River bridge on the edge of the city, he arrived in Murphysboro just "when the tornado struck. The wind began to whistle through the cab," he said.

> And the engine was pelted with flying boards. Then we saw the terrific funnel-shaped cloud approach from the west and saw houses tumbling before it. The air was full of wreckage. As we passed the shoe factory [Brown Shoe Company on Nineteenth Street] in the south end of town, the train was so bombarded by heavy planks . . . that I was afraid some of them would pierce the boiler. They struck with such force they made the engine quiver.
>
> We kept going, sometimes plowing through the wreckage that threatened to block us, and by the time we reached the center of town the full force of the storm was upon us. Bodies were lying in the streets and buildings everywhere were being demolished. To make matters worse . . . a big grain elevator [the Reliance Mill] caved in on the track and we couldn't get out of the tornado's path. We had to stay there until after 5 o'clock and several times during the wait were forced to fight hard to keep the train from catching fire [railroad cars of the era were predominantly made of wood] from blazes that broke out in the piles of debris along the track.

Through it all, people were running about in a state of panic. The most awful thing I have ever seen. We saw many being carried on stretchers or dragged from the burning remains of buildings. The fire department was helpless because the storm had broken all the water mains. Fire swept the Blue Front Hotel. We were told that several persons lost their lives.

I saw [amazing] displays of heroism . . . but I want to mention one case in particular. That was the work of the [N]egro cook at the Blue Front Hotel. After he had been cut and burned until he hardly looked like a human being, he worked like a demon for two hours, carrying out the dead and injured and was still working when we finally got the track cleared and left town.[12]

North of the Blue Front, the ruins of Reliance Mills smoldered as did the wholesale warehouses of the Borgsmiller family, the Blue Grass Creamery, Standard Oil, and the Anchor Ice Plant.

The Blue Front Hotel sat right across Walnut Street from the M&O depot, a pattern of public lodging construction seen in most railroad towns of the era simply because proximity to the depot meant passengers debarking from a train would have easy access. This was an era when traveling salesmen, or as they were sometimes known in the day, hustlers, got off trains with grips full of their wares—glass for the table, shoes, hats, clothing, and the like—and set up displays in special rooms designed for the purpose. Built in 1908, the Laclede Hotel, at Ninth and Chestnut Streets, is the last of six period hotels standing today. The property was widely known for its commodious display rooms. The Maryland Hotel, a competitor, was right across the street from the M&O depot at Seventeenth and Walnut. The Logan Hotel, built in 1889, was on the west side of courthouse square, and the M&O Hotel was within easy walking distance, too.

When the storm hit, panicked guests fled to the Blue Front's basement. The building collapsed trapping them under tons of brick and rubble. Ignited by the cookstoves in the kitchen, dry building timbers and lath from plastered walls became the tinder for an immolating fire that spread quickly.

Engineer Kiley's account does not mention his train would perform a mercy mission by carrying away scores of the injured, most of whom were taken to St. Mary's Hospital in East St. Louis, Illinois, the city that Kiley and his family called home. Later on, Barnes Hospital in St. Louis would accept Murphysboro overflow patients. Much like the lists of war dead and casualties from World War I eight years before, the front page of the *Murphysboro Daily Republican* ran a daily list of dead and injured furnished by a Murphysboro surgeon, Dr. R. S. Sabine, who oversaw the forty-six Murphysboro patients' physical condition while they were in Barnes Hospital. Eleven on the list were children.[13] In addition, a special IC train carried fifty-one injured to St. Louis, forty from St. Andrew's Hospital in Murphysboro, seven from the temporary hospital in the Eagles Club, and four from the Masonic Temple.[14] Not a dime was billed for the service by either railroad.

Yet another engineer, E. Bonton of the Missouri-Pacific, said, "I have seen hurricanes in the West Indies, but I have never seen any wind that did such damage as that at Murphysboro. And when the wind quit, the fires began. I saw a man carrying a little girl with both her legs off."[15]

Staff correspondent Sam O'Neill of the *St. Louis Post-Dispatch* interviewed May Williams from the St. Louis suburb of Cheltenham in the Dogtown area. She was in Murphysboro that Wednesday in early afternoon to stage an old-fashioned revival meeting at the Moose Lodge. Wednesday in Egypt is a church day second only in attendance and importance to the Sabbath. Williams, the evangelist for the revival, was staying at the Logan Hotel. She often volunteered time to the Whosoever Mission, the sponsors of the revival.

The meeting barely underway, the roof ripped off the Moose Lodge, exposing a sky filled with whirling objects. "I closed my eyes," she said, when the back wall collapsed out, and the roof began to cave in on her and the troupe. "Suddenly from the bottom of one of the stoves which heated the hall came a great puff and the flames burst out like tongues of fire. There was . . . an explosion and the other stove was broken. The whole place rocked."

Williams and a fellow Nazarene saint, Sister Parrott, walked out into the bedlam that was Murphysboro, in hopes of getting to the safety of a home of a parishioner they both knew. "We . . . heard terrible cries, yells, screams," Mrs. Williams told the reporter,

> and there were great popping noises. The world roared. The storm passed. There were still cries but it seemed almost silent. People were praying out loud. Young boys and girls ran up to us crying. . . . [T]hey couldn't find their mothers, their fathers, or their sisters. The air was filled with the cries of . . . people under wreckage. People walked the streets bleeding from wounds crying wildly the names of missing loved ones as they looked for their families. Everything was on fire it seemed . . . no light except that from the . . . flames. There was no water.

The air was filled with black smoke and red-hot sparks. "We were black from head to foot," she said.[16]

That first night temperatures fell to 38°F. The next night brought a reading of 29°F. Those who had relatives with homes yet standing found shelter there, and others left town. But with no place to stay and no agencies to turn to for immediate relief, eight thousand homeless Murphysboro citizens heard ambulance bells ringing and breathed the smoke fouling the crisp night air from the fires burning what was left of their lives. They flinched when dynamite charges that the National Guard set off to prevent the spread of the fires chafed already-raw nerves. Survivors made grim searches for their dead in temporary morgues and hospitals. Many of those who lost homes gathered in a field on the west side of town, lighting bonfires to stave off the chill, those fires stoked with wood that was someone's home mere hours before.

Lying on an army cot in that special IC medical train, Elsie Rathert was interviewed by the *Benton (IL) Evening News*. Her father, Albert, a bricklayer by trade, was by her side. Elsie was on the way to Union Station in St. Louis and then to Barnes Hospital a short distance away. She had been at her neighbors visiting. "The house toppled and I found myself [under] a heavy plank," she told the Benton reporter. "When I looked down and tried to get up . . . I felt of my left leg and found it smashed very badly. I pulled it out all crushed and broken and held it aside while a neighbor helped me

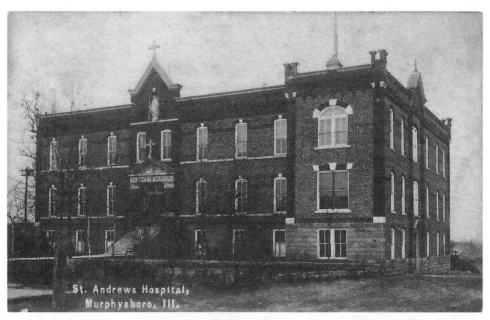

St. Andrew's Hospital, Murphysboro, Illinois, ca. 1907. *From a penny postcard in the author's collection.*

out. Yes, sir, they cut off what was left of my . . . leg. I will never walk again. I will be a cripple for life."[17] The irony of her sad story is that her own home was virtually unscathed.

Try as the volunteer medical professionals might, gangrene quickly became a problem. Madeline Wagner Will was pregnant with her first child. She related to an interviewer in 1993 that her "father had been blown over what was left of the house and about half a city block into a neighbor's yard. Around midnight the ambulance came and got Dad. He had internal injuries. His back was black and blue and his leg broke." He was carried to the new Eagles Club building downtown. "Dad ended up taking gangrene and died two days later."[18] The first terrible hours were not the cleanliest. Mrs. Will's memory tells a story not at all uncommon in a time when penicillin was unavailable and would not be until the end of World War II. In Murphysboro alone, 363 gangrene cases were reported.[19]

In 1895 a serious railroad accident brought the realization to the community that a permanent hospital was needed. Although the injured received good care from two Franciscan sisters from Belleville, both of whom were teachers in the St. Andrew's School, a committee was soon organized, plans were drawn for a twenty-nine-bed Catholic hospital, and 146 people collected $9,234.79 for the building fund. Two years later, the Franciscan Sisters of Wheaton, Illinois, opened the new facility and would operate it until 1956. For a patient in 1897, a private room scaled from $7 to $10 a week. In the aftermath of the tornado, St. Andrew's admitted 187 injured, of whom 37 died. One surgeon performed thirty-two leg amputations and thirteen skull operations in the first twenty-four hours, most of which were accomplished with only coal-oil lamps for light. The sixteen nuns on duty brought milk and cookies to the children.[20]

Reporter Fred Gardner sent a special dispatch from St. Andrew's to the *St. Louis Globe-Democrat* for March 20 publication telling of "children lying in huddled groups amid suffering and groans of the wounded. Disfigured faces, broken limbs, and bodies and wailing relatives filled the hospital from the basement to the third floor. Six children died before midnight, and others lay at the point of death."

The reporter also visited the Murphysboro American Legion Post, which had become a hospital and temporary morgue, where he saw "[l]ittle Suzanne who has but one tuft of curly hair peeping from the cotton swathing about her head. Wrapped in a blanket [on her cot] and sipping grape juice from a bottle, little Suzanne does not know her mother and daddy are dead. She does not know her brother is dying. Soon Suzanne will be all alone."

The nuns running St. Andrew's were so busy they missed a man sitting quietly in a closet for twenty hours before anyone saw him. The dazed patient was diagnosed with a fractured skull and a serious concussion.

Some injured were transported to Carbondale by an IC passenger train engineered by Edward Whalen. They went to Holden Hospital; two refrigerated cars carried the dead to the National Guard Armory.

Medical personnel as well as ordinary people were no doubt both amused and relieved to hear that none other than Percy Owens, chief Prohibition enforcement agent for the state of Illinois, cabled the Murphysboro Relief Committee to inform them that "a supply of confiscated liquor would be placed at their disposal if they can find a use for it. It was stated the offer will probably be accepted."[21]

Not enough can be said about the medical professionals who came to the aid of a beaten and battered people. From Chicago, Cairo, Anna, Carbondale, and Marion, Illinois, and St. Louis, volunteers appeared to heal Egypt.

"At the Elks Club," wrote Stannard for the *Post-Dispatch* March 20 edition,

Doctor J. E. Rein of Chicago stood beside a cot and saw Evelyn Smith, 8 years old. She was crushed in a cave-in during the tornado. Her thigh bone was fractured. After lying for some hours in the chilling rain, she was taken to the rescue station [where] Dr. Rein treated her [even though] her case was hopeless. Suffering from the fractures, and exposure, [Evelyn] contracted pneumonia. Dr. Rein, haggard from the work of the operating room found time to visit the cot often and for thirty-six hours on end devoted every spare minute to his little patient. Yesterday morning he was persuaded to go to bed but arose only after fifteen minutes and returned to her bedside. Yesterday at noon, Evelyn died.

The March 23 extra edition of the *Murphysboro Daily Independent* carried a painfully personal advertisement: "Mrs. George Launis nee Dorothy Webb is missing. Anyone knowing her whereabouts is requested to notify Gus Rathgeber at once." The following day the newspaper reported, "Charred Body Claimed Today From Roberts Morgue is that of Mrs. Dorothy Webb Launis, 1911 Gartside St." In a sack, the horribly burned body of a woman lay unidentified, the only such casualty unclaimed in the city five days after the tornado. "The trunk remained, limbs and arms were taken by the fire. So, today a surgeon resorted to the one remaining way of identifying the unfortunate . . . an operation. Men with grim faces witnessed the identification." Dorothy was pregnant with the couple's first child.

NIGHT

That first night, fire and death roamed Murphysboro hand in hand. Security in the city of Murphysboro was a major concern. Immediately after the storm, Major Robert W. Davis of the Illinois National Guard stationed at Carbondale, after receiving orders from Governor Len Small, took charge of Murphysboro. Davis's unit, Company K, of the 130th US Infantry Regiment, 3rd Battalion, had been formed in 1728 and had been commanded in earlier years by George Washington and George Rogers Clark. The 130th fought with distinction in all armed conflicts down to World War I, when Major Davis and his battalion saw action at the Somme, Lorraine, Picardy, and the Meuse-Argonne, arguably one of the bloodiest battles in this country's history. His peacetime occupation was copublisher of the *Carbondale Free Press*.

Major Davis's first actions were to close all entrances to the battered city, post armed guards at all banks and jewelry stores, and offer logistical support, bringing experienced battlefield organizational skills to search-and-rescue efforts. By Saturday, military tents, cots, and blankets transported by rail from Chicago on the IC were in place to shelter the estimated eight thousand refugees. Sixty-five army tents arrayed in orderly rows were erected across the street from the high school. By early May, the tents were being disassembled for return to the military.[22]

Men standing next to an army-issue tent. Nearly everything within eyesight is gone. *Photo courtesy of the West Franklin (Illinois) Historical District and Silkwood Inn Museum.*

To reduce the threat of looting in the near-total destruction, Major Davis deputized two hundred men to patrol for looters. Thirty people were arrested and slapped in the Jackson County jail. Often, husbands stood guard over what was left of their family's material world. The first night four men were arrested on suspicions they were attempting to loot. One man found stripping wedding rings from deceased wives' fingers had his head beaten in with a board by an irate policeman.

One of Major Davis's lieutenants took peacekeeping a little too zealously. At 11:00 A.M. Friday, Will Morgan, "a colored musician," was ordered to leave the porch of a "resort" on Bridge Street.[23] Morgan refused to comply so the militia lieutenant shot him through the leg. Sheriff C. E. White, in a jurisdictional dustup, alleged the shooting was unprovoked and personally drove Morgan by patrol car to St. Mary's for treatment. Murphysboro was hardly singular with looting issues. In DeSoto, east of Murphysboro and also hit by the tornado, "[t]he looters and the ransackers arrived early, as well as the curious." West Frankfort's chief of police Charles Norman told the newspaper that auto thefts were more than in the six months previous to the tornado.[24]

The *Daily Independent* ran regular, front-page warnings of the very real dangers to be found in Murphysboro, like the March 26 one under the headline "CO-OPERATION FOR LAW ENFORCEMENT."

> Owing to conditions of this city on account of men of all character swarming in for anything they might find to do that is unlawful or mean, we are particularly making an effort to protect any of the citizens that might fall as their prey and especially girls and young women of the city. These men are men of characters such that they have no respect for women and we are desirous to have the help of the citizens to this end, and in asking you to co-operate with us we are asking parents and guardians to keep girls and young women off the streets after 7 o'clock in the evening unless they are properly and safely escorted. We are going to do all in our power to protect them, but there will be instances when we will miss them and by doing this it may have some embarrassment and probably in some instances things that might be serious.
>
> C. E. White, Sheriff
> Joe Boston, Chief of Police
> Robert W. Davis, Major, Commanding Troops

The *St. Louis Post Dispatch* the day after the Tri-State reported, "Dynamite was used here last night to stop the fires of the blazing element. Among the buildings raised [*sic*] by charges of the explosive was the Elks Majestic Club." Major Davis's men laid and set off the charges. Murphysboro had become Dante's Inferno.

With no electricity to power civic water pumps, firefighters from many towns had only picks and shovels for tools. The city of Herrin sent a brand-new fire truck, which was crushed when a blazing brick wall collapsed on it.[25]

Eileen Breeden Jones was in second grade at Washington School in a class forty-seven pupils large. "[We were] out on the playground," she said in a voice scraped by time.

> I can't remember seeing a cloud or anything but I heard one of the teachers say to the other, "I think we ought take these kids inside." And they said, "Maybe we better." So we started to go into the school building and somebody said, "No, go into the basement." And that's where we started. Just as we were going down the steps, the storm hit. And bricks fell in around us. I'm thankful to say that there were some that were hit but not bad and I didn't get any of them. And, then . . . then some.

Eileen hesitated, her hands tumbling on themselves in her lap as she searched for words dredged from a tortured remembrance.

> Then, from then on it was just chaos. The teachers and all were carrying on and I don't know where my Dad was. They sent my Uncle Harold to the school and he come in that school building teachers all grabbed him 'round the neck and was hangin' on to him but he was after me and he took me home then. The rest of that day, well, it was just chaotic. All I can say.

Distracted, Eileen cleared her throat and gazed at her hands balled in a knot in her lap.

> We lived next door to my grandmother who had a little grocery store, and I had an aunt and uncle up the street from us. We were all at my Gramma's house. We had got word for everybody to grab a change of clothes. And keep 'em handy, 'cause the fires was comin', and we'd have to cross the river [the Big Muddy on the eastern edge of the city] and that was the way we spent the day, but all you could hear all day was things a-blowin' up, they were dynamitin'. And tryin' to stop the fires and all that. And along in the afternoon my Dad come

to the door and said, "I need a change of clothes." My mother, she said, "What's the matter?" "Why," he said, "I was goin' through some yards, an outside toilet had blown away," and he said, "I stepped in it." So he had to come home, change his clothes and then he left.[26]

The very next morning, like the mythic Phoenix, Murphysboro began to rise from the ashes. Volunteers helped with the discovery and removal of bodies, cleaned streets, moved fallen power poles, and sorted through the ruins in hopes of finding bits and pieces of the past in the debris field. Reporter Stannard told of a "well-dressed woman . . . seen rummaging into a pile of wreckage that was her home. She reaches a bureau half buried, takes from a top drawer an armful of linens and walks away with the air of having found the one treasure she was needing."

Shell-shocked people wandered the streets. Since the winds had torn the clothing right off many of their backs, townspeople dressed in whatever could be scavenged. Men wearing women's coats and women with male garb created an other-worldly unisex pathos to the scene. It was often difficult to guess which gender a child was from what he or she wore: "Many boys were forced to wear dresses until a proper trade could be made."[27]

In Murphysboro, the only town in the Tri-State's path that allowed black people to live within its city limits, news of the injured and dead was parsed

A Murphysboro family visiting what is left of their home. *Photo courtesy of the West Franklin (Illinois) Historical District and Silkwood Inn Museum.*

by race in the papers, as two examples from the March 27 *Daily Independent* show: "Storm Victims in St. Andrews [hospital], the Injuries, Arquilla WADE, colored, severe burns," and in another listing embedded in a depressingly long roll call of Murphysboro dead, "Mrs. JONES and Mrs. SLATER, colored; Dolph ISOM, colored; Mrs. KELLY, colored."

Another tragic incident a week and a half after the tornado was also reported in the March 27 *Daily Independent*.

> Granville Whitelaw, colored, 60 years old, came through the tornado March 18, and . . . found himself living in a refuge[e] tent with others of his race, on North 17th Street. At 7 P.M., a terrific lightning and rain storm broke over the devastated city. When it passed, Whitelaw was found a corpse, a victim of the lightning. Whitelaw had lived here for years. The "thunderbolt" that laid the old man low, caused superstitions to rise again through the encampment of colored storm refugees here, few of whom slept for hours after Whitelaw's death was reported.

The Ku Klux Klan chapter also used the local newspaper to communicate with its members. With its regional epicenter in Marion and Herrin in next-door Williamson County, the Ku Klux Klan operated freely in southern Illinois in 1925. Egypt's mission was mainly directed at policing Prohibition, putting a stranglehold on bootlegging, and corralling the widespread corruption attendant to illegal alcohol distribution. The Klan was vehemently anti-Catholic and believed in the separation of the races and that miscegenation was a capital crime. On March 26, 1925, the following notice ran in the *Daily Independent*: "Knights of the Ku Klux Klan are requested to register at Crossfield's Variety Store. We want correct information as well as financial loss to the membership. Whether you sustained any loss or not, please register at once.—Liberty Klan No. 131."

With little or no fanfare, several railroads backed Pullman cars onto recently cleared sidings to accommodate visiting relief workers and medical personnel from St. Louis, Cairo, and Chicago. The M&O and the IC offered refugees pro bono passage anywhere on their railroads. "Temporary kitchens . . . [were] set up in the streets and fraternal organization facilities. A commissary train arrived Wednesday night with a supply of food. The residents are being fed from these places and from various railway dining cars which came with the commissary train."[28]

A twenty-five-year-old reporter from the Bloomington *Pantagraph* rode south on the Illinois Central's crack passenger train, the Panama Limited.

The young journalist, Adlai Stevenson, whose family owned a significant percentage of the newspaper, had flunked out of Harvard Law School the previous summer but later became governor of Illinois, ran two times for president, and served as the US ambassador to the United Nations during the troubled times of the Cold War that included helping the John F. Kennedy administration to defuse the Cuban Missile Crisis.

From aboard this train, Stevenson, in his first dispatch for the March 20 edition, stated, "An atmosphere of catastrophe and havoc pervades all trains en route to the storm-stricken area. The train is carrying three cars of volunteer nurses and doctors, many of whom saw service on the muddy fields of Flanders and know, without being told, something of what awaits." He was referring to the 108th Medical Regiment from Chicago.

The first damaged community he saw was DeSoto. Six miles south, he disembarked in Carbondale to make his way to the devastation of Murphysboro, which he described: "Viewing the broad expanse of scattered, twisted smoldering wreckage, one cannot but reflect on the futility of life and the insignificance of man."

"Many doctors have not taken off their aprons in 36 hours," Stevenson said in the March 21 edition. Surgeons used boards lain across sawhorses as operating tables, and a bucket of boiled water at their feet sufficed to sterilize instruments. "The few available hearses," he reported, "are racing back and forth to the cemetery, carrying two caskets at a time, many of them small ones. Of formal funerals there are none, but of heroic fortitude there is much."

Stannard with the *St. Louis Post-Dispatch* filed his report on Saturday, three days after the storm: "Rescue workers are still digging and now and then a rushing ambulance or a jogging wagon bearing away a body to the morgue tells the story of another gruesome find."

In his final report, Stevenson described a scene likely witnessed in front of the Masonic Lodge or the Elks Club, substantial buildings in what was left of the commercial district near the courthouse square that served as both hospital and morgue: "I saw a farmer dressed in his best suit, pale but dry-eyed and composed, push his way thru a crowd in front of a morgue and emerge later carrying a tiny white casket. The crowd gave way in reverent awe and closed behind him intent on its own business. He placed the casket tenderly beside him in his Ford and drove away."[29] Stevenson would learn that the casket was for two-year-old Mary. The farmer's baby, Jane, was still inside the morgue. The death rolls contain a May Dell Martin, two, and a Madeline Martin, three months. Perhaps the names were transcribed inaccurately (see appendix).

Elks Home, Murphysboro, Ill.—3

Murphysboro Elks Club Lodge 572, built in 1916 on Walnut Street. It was used as a temporary triage center, hospital, and morgue. *From a postcard, ca. 1920, in the author's collection.*

Stevenson also saw a "big, strapping, fine looking miner" who opened a "cheap watch and gaze[d] with tear-rimmed eyes at the photo of a girl inside." The miner showed the watch to a militiaman on guard duty and asked, "That's my Ruth, is she inside?" "No," and "away he goes on his fruitless search."[30]

On Sunday, newspapermen, soldiers acting as traffic cops, and others close to the turmoil estimated that sixty thousand people visited Murphysboro to get a glimpse at what was left of the city.[31]

Morticians from surrounding towns were brought in to prepare the dead. This included a black undertaker from Carbondale. In makeshift morgues throughout the city, women set to work to wash bodies that awaited burial. Death was far more personal in 1925 than today.

Wilma Theiss (later Kimmel) spent the summer in Murphysboro worrying about her father, Johannes "John" Konrad Theiss IV, who had been an engineer for the Gartside Coal Company No. 4. Gartside shuttered its doors. Too few customers were left to justify staying in business. Her father's leg injury required his removal on the M&O to Barnes Hospital in St. Louis. He returned in late June but could find only part-time work at Central Illinois Public Service, the local electric utility, and was in and out of several jobs.

"Papa began to realize," Mrs. Kimmel said in an interview, "if he were to find another line of work, he'd have to leave Murphysboro as many people already had." A relative found him a job as a machinist in East St. Louis. "He was to work there till 1947." The idea of leaving was "difficult" for her mother, but the inevitable day came, and "she was never again to know the life she had before the tornado."

Clara Bell Hartmann Theiss, Mrs. Kimmel's mother, had been separated from her beloved family and hometown and was brought back to

A temporary morgue in Murphysboro, Illinois, containing nine corpses in what looks to be a railroad warehouse. The man on the right, probably looking for a loved one, has pulled back a shroud to look at the face of a corpse. Chicago Daily News *photo negative collection, DN-0079918; image courtesy of the Chicago History Museum.*

A typical street scene after crews have had a chance to move debris. The nicely crowned street is paved with Egyptian brand bricks made by the Murphysboro Paving Brick Company. *Photo courtesy of the West Franklin (Illinois) Historical District and Silkwood Inn Museum.*

Murphysboro to be cared for by the same physician who had seen to her family's medical needs for three decades. She succumbed to cancer in April 1928 surrounded by her family rather than on the unfamiliar streets of East St. Louis.[32]

In an hour-long meeting convened in his private railcar on March 20, the *Daily Independent* told readers, M&O Railroad vice president Norris pledged to the Relief Committee and its chairman, attorney Ike Levy, the M&O repair facilities would be rehabilitated. "We are beginning at once the rebuilding of the roundhouse here in Murphysboro," he said. "We shall also begin at once the replacement of our large reclamation shop here." Four days later Norris was quoted in the same newspaper, "Murphysboro is our work headquarters north of the [Ohio] river. It is vitally necessary to us. This is our heaviest division. We have for a long time made cars here and shall continue to make them here."

This statement would prove deceiving. Three days after Christmas, Murphysboro was informed the locomotive shop was to be moved in a "centralization" strategy to Jackson, Tennessee. The reposition mimicked what their substantially larger competitor the IC had done with its locomotive repair facility by moving it to Paducah, Kentucky, in 1923.

Adding further competitive pressure, in January 1925, the IC announced a $6 million build-out of the rail yard to include a car repair shed, blacksmith shop, carpenter shop, a wood mill, and a storeroom. Management at the M&O claimed the storm had nothing whatsoever to do with the corporate decision to move from Murphysboro. The day after the announcement, the city awoke doubly chilled. That morning the thermometer read six below zero.

On Friday civic leaders gathered at the Elks Club. Clearly, the extent of the city-wide damage demanded a coordinated plan implemented with skill and attention to detail. Murphysboro needed a relief agenda and a committee to ensure the agenda was executed properly. Governor Len Small was in the city viewing storm damage. During the meeting, with a trembling voice and tears welled up in his eyes, he pledged the resources of the State. Governor Small returned to Springfield to champion a $500,000 relief package that was quickly and unanimously approved by both houses of the General Assembly.[33]

When the tornado blew through, Isaac Levy was pleading a case in the Union County Courthouse in Jonesboro, south of Murphysboro, a location not far from where Abraham Lincoln debated Stephen A. Douglas in the 1858 US Senate election. Levy was elected chairman of the Relief Committee. Both the committee and Levy were to perform an enormous service to the city. He announced after the votes were counted that he thought it necessary to issue a general statement to the nation. The assembled voiced their approval.

Already prepared, he read from a typed sheet pulled from an inside pocket of his suit coat.

> To the Public—In behalf of the citizens of Murphysboro and vicinity, accept our sincere thanks and grateful appreciation for everything you did for us following the destructive storm of March 18th. The many acts of love and kindness and the many sacrifices that were made following this terrible disaster demonstrate that regardless of creed and distance, we are after all akin and bound by the closest ties. Your generous and timely assistance has given us new hope, much courage, and great confidence in the future of Murphysboro. Your kindly acts at a time when we were prostrate and helpless shall never be forgotten. The citizens of Murphysboro and vicinity feel deeply grateful and thankful for every assistance rendered them. We are distressed, but are greatly encouraged, and a city that has the spirit that we possess is bound to succeed. May God bless you all for everything you are doing for us.[34]

On Sunday, more than one hundred victims were buried at Tower Grove and St. Andrew's cemeteries on a hill overlooking what the storm did not spare. Eighty gravediggers worked from dawn to dusk.[35] "Grave diggers in overhauls [sic] rested on their shovels at times to act as pall bearers while [collections] of sorrowing people watch[ed] their loved ones being lowered into their graves," reported Associated Press reporter E. N. Shunk, who had been given a note handwritten by Levy granting Shunk liberty to roam the ruins. The pass was written in pencil.

Of the ten churches in the distraught city, only a handful was intact, the largest of which was St. Andrew's Catholic Church, next to the hospital. Three Masses were held that morning open to all. Sensing this was not enough to assuage the city's depth of despair, Levy called for a memorial service on Courthouse Square next to the Jackson County Courthouse and jail. At a grandstand left unscathed by the winds and near an ensign-less flagpole bent in a c-shape all the way to the pavement, Murphysboro attempted to find some solace.

Old jail (*left*) and courthouse in Murphysboro. The courthouse was built in the Second Empire style popular in mid-nineteenth-century America for commercial, governmental, and upscale single-family residences. Brownsville—a ghost town now—was the first Jackson County seat of government, whose courthouse was erected in 1816 and burned to the ground in 1843, twenty-seven years to the day after its completion. The county seat was moved to Murphysboro. *Postcard in the author's collection.*

With "the clang of hearse and ambulance and fire wagon" to echo their distress, on a "sunlit March day," each of Murphysboro's pastors was given a chance to lay a calming hand on the hearts of the gathered, including the Reverend J. A. McFall of the African Methodist Episcopal Church, who informed the crowd Murphysboro had lost twenty-three African American citizens and that he came to the memorial service to offer his people's cooperation.

"Two thousand stood there," wrote a staff reporter for the March 23 *Daily Independent*. "Mothers and fathers, some homeless, some children, eyes wet and eyes too dry to cry. While they were told of the amaze of the nation that a people, their dead yet unburied, could turn with such determination to the rebuilding of abode and place of industry." *Nearer My God to Thee* and *Rock of Ages* were sung.

In a June 15 letter to Levy, Henry M. Baker, Red Cross national disaster relief director stationed at regional headquarters in Carbondale, enumerated

The public funeral service held on Courthouse Square, Sunday, March 22, 1925. *Photo courtesy of the Jackson County Historical Society of Illinois.*

Destruction in Murphysboro's northeastern corner as the tornado sped out of town toward DeSoto. *Photo courtesy of the West Franklin (Illinois) Historical District and Silkwood Inn Museum.*

the progress that had been made in Murphysboro in the three months since the Tri-State: 707 houses were repaired, 204 houses rebuilt, and 238 houses were under construction. To that point in the relief effort, over $900,000 had been spent in Egypt by the Red Cross.[36] Triple that figure would be expended over time, but it would not be enough.

Notwithstanding the hopeful statements, despite the labor and expenditure of fortunes, Murphysboro would never be the same.

3

▼

DeSoto, Illinois

Just seven minutes after most of Murphysboro was leveled, the Tri-State Tornado hit DeSoto at 2:48 P.M. No town in the path would proportionally suffer a higher fatality rate than this tiny village in which sixty-nine people died. Thirty-three of them were children buried in the burning ruins of the DeSoto Schoolhouse, a heartbreaking record that remains the single worst tornado-related death toll for a school in US history. One in four DeSoto children who walked off to school that day would never come home to supper.

Like scenes from Nagasaki and Hiroshima, for as far as the eye could see almost nothing remained intact. In a June 15, 1925, report addressed to "All members of all advisory committees" affected by the DeSoto disaster, Henry M. Baker of the Red Cross wrote, "All homes and businesses [are] completely destroyed" including the schoolhouse, which was valued at $20,000. The town carried no insurance on the property. The only good news in the report was that all five teachers and the principal escaped with their lives.[1]

The small town of five hundred was a farming community where the IC maintained an active depot to carry the town's wheat, hay, Irish potatoes, strawberries, and peanuts to urban markets, yet it was coal mining that provided the largest number of jobs. Most of the men worked in Bush at Western Coal No. 1, a shaft mine open since 1903. Still others worked a primitive strip mine in Elkville, one town north on State Route 2 in an operation that used mule- or horse-drawn scrapers to expose the coal seam. Jackson County listed seventeen open or operating coal mines in 1925. Most

DeSoto, Illinois. The ten autos and one truck lined up on Illinois Route 2 face south. An Illinois Central train is stopped where the depot once stood. *Photo courtesy of the West Franklin (Illinois) Historical District and Silkwood Inn Museum.*

DeSoto the day after the tornado. The area is still smoldering. The men to the right are standing in the ruins of Frank Redd's store, where Redd and his wife burned to death. *From a panorama photograph credited to Wieh of Greenville, Illinois; courtesy of the White County (Illinois) Historical Society.*

RNADO AND FIRE WED.MARCH 18·1925.

More of the panorama credited to Wieh, depicting the ruins of the Albon State Bank, predecessor to the Bank of DeSoto. The homes northwest of downtown have been completely erased. *Photo courtesy of the White County (Illinois) Historical Society.*

were shaft mines, but one, the Black Servant Mine—in 1921 owned by a consortium of investors out of Harrisburg, Illinois—was the first to use an electrically powered shovel, or in modern parlance, drag line, to strip mine coal near Elkville. DeSoto miners worked as far away as West Frankfort, twenty-three miles to the northeast. Yet, despite technological innovation at the Black Servant and the use of electricity rather than steam power in above-ground operations, in 1925 a few mines still used mules to haul coal from the seam face to the hoist.

Charles Dickens could hardly have approved of boys as young as twelve allowed underground, but it was the norm in an Egypt in which on-site mine inspectors did indeed carry canaries into the tangle of shafts every day the operation was open to sense when methane gas had reached lethal levels. DeSoto was spared the odoriferous problem of spontaneously combusted gob piles, which were heaps of nonsalable mine tailings that other southern Illinois towns endured with mines nearby or even, as was the case in West Frankfort and Zeigler, contiguous to the miners' homes. Some gob piles burned twenty-four hours a day with a sickly yellow flame stained with blue, adding a sulphurous stink to the already acrid coal smoke fouling the air produced by heating and cooking stoves, boiler systems, kilns, railroads, and furnaces.

DeSoto's Martin Barnett hauled coal with a team of horses to provide a part of his family's living. Perhaps he hauled for the Kathleen Mine in

Dowell, two towns north. The mine promised "satisfaction, clean, sootless, clinkerless" coal "prepared in uniform size. Nut Coal delivered—$5.00 [a ton]; Furnace Lump, delivered—$5.50; Large Lump, delivered—$6.00; Yard and Office, 422 So. Washington, Hundley Coal Co., telephone 231" in Carbondale.[2]

The year 1925 was the zenith of coal production in Egypt due to depletion of reserves, national increases in the consumption of petroleum and natural gas, and the ascendance of electricity production and usage.[3] One also cannot underestimate hesitancy on the part of investors to begin new ventures in unionized southern Illinois coalfields notoriously prone to strikes and deadly violence. Too many miners had died already. Too many fortunes had been lost to strikes and walkouts.

In 1910, nonunion mines had finally been run out of business in the heavily immigrant-worked coalfields of Zeigler, Illinois, where DeSoto men often found jobs. The mine was owned by the Leiter family of Chicago, whose wealth was created by Levi Zeigler Leiter when he established the predecessor store to Marshall Field and Company, the sale proceeds of which were invested in rapidly appreciating Chicago real estate. The mine was the idea of his son, Joseph. After Levi died in 1904, his widow, Mary, held controlling interest. She closed and then sold the mining operation after a series of methane explosions killed ninety-two miners during a six-year period. The closing ended lethal pressure the United Mine Workers (UMW) had exerted since 1904. Physical threat was so severe Leiter was forced to fortify the mine with a sturdy stockade around the property as well as blockhouses positioned along the perimeter armed with men toting machine guns and equipped with military-quality searchlights.

As recent as 1923, deadly labor problems erupted in Egypt. In a strip mine halfway between Herrin and Marion in Williamson County where DeSoto men also worked, scabs recruited from unemployment agencies in Chicago by a neophyte West Virginia mine owner, W. J. Lester, were hired to replace striking UMW members. Twenty-three unarmed strikers under the truce of a white flag died gruesome deaths at the hands of a union mob. All six defendants were acquitted. The juries blamed Lester for the tragedy. The decision was roundly denounced in the national media.

A moving excerpt from a 1984 interview was given by eighty-three-year-old Marie South Williams, a DeSoto native who left town after high school to pursue a teaching career.

Of course in Carterville [a small town twelve miles southeast of DeSoto], I saw a load of them [black men], seven of them killed and throwed into a wagon. They had come to break the strike, you know.

They was going to put them Negroes to work. And the union men met them on the south side of town . . . killed seven . . . and just throwed the[m] . . . on top of each other and took them to Dewmaine,[4] a little town that was nothing but Negroes that worked there. And just throwed them out on the street. And I happened to be uptown after school . . . a bunch of us . . . and saw them drive by.[5]

There can be no doubt that sophisticated investors were beginning to avoid investment in new mines after hearing of the brutality of the unions and their proclivity to strike.

The coal economy of DeSoto supported a flour mill north of town, a lumberyard, a grain elevator, a drugstore faced with fancy, yellow ceramic tiles that also offered soda-fountain service, a barbershop, two small restaurants, a cobbler, a livery stable, a bank, and two general stores, both housed in substantial brick buildings. One of them was Frank Redd's two-story affair at the corner of Main Street and State Route 2. The Odd Fellows hall upstairs reflected an era in America when both men and women belonged to a long list of social organizations whose guiding spirits were as diversified as their goals. The other general store was the larger Walker and Albon's, which sold groceries, men's suits, furniture, clothing, and fresh meats and at one time acted as the only bank in town. Ice cut from the frozen Big Muddy River just east of town could be bought from the back room of one of the restaurants. A sheet-metal grain elevator on the east side of the IC tracks later served as a relief depot where people from the area could drop off clothing for the tornado's refugees, one of whom was a widowed mother and her five children walking from East Cape Girardeau, Illinois, to Effingham, Illinois, a distance of 160 miles.

DESOTO'S LOSSES

A horrifying 14 percent of DeSoto's population died shocking deaths. One report by Samuel O'Neil, staff correspondent for the *St. Louis Post-Dispatch*, who was sent by car to cover the disaster, mentioned seeing only a dozen buildings still standing in DeSoto and that airmen from Scott Field in Belleville, Illinois, were "working to relieve the survivors. . . . Frank Redd and his wife were trapped in their general store when it collapsed and was destroyed by fire."[6] They did not escape. The couple was buried side by side in the Oakland Cemetery in Carbondale.

Jackson County Deputy Sheriff George Boland was last seen by his family as he sailed away, sucked into the blackness of the wind, lifted and spun in the fouled air like so much dust. Boland was never seen again.

Nearly half of the town's dead were children who lost their lives in the DeSoto School. A shaken thirteen-year-old Garrett Crews survived the collapse of the building.

> So, I was looking out the school window [of the second floor] . . . and at the last moment you could see the air full of debris or whatever, just houses and pieces of everything. About the time I saw all this, our teacher instructed us to put the windows down. And we did. The windows was on the west side . . . [a]nd I remember . . . going over there, and being six feet tall . . . I put my hands up to the very top . . . I [was] praying . . . that's the last thing I remember.

Dazed, perhaps in shock, he left the school grounds: "On my way . . . to where my house was, or, as it turned out, where it had been, I was about halfway there, in front of another house that had been blown away, and the people who lived in this house were standing there in the yard. And the father was holding a very young child in his arms, and as I recall it, the infant was either dead or died in his arms in my presence."[7]

Eight-year-old Betty Barnett lived on the corner of Cherry Street and the Lincoln Highway, today's Illinois Route 149. Her father, Martin, had a

Seven army-issue tents, in what is left of DeSoto, erected by homeowners on the sites of their houses. *Photo courtesy of the West Franklin (Illinois) Historical District and Silkwood Inn Museum.*

horse-drawn wagon to haul coal or anything else people wanted, including heavy items delivered to the IC depot. The family of seven supplemented their pantry with a large vegetable garden. Minnie Barnett, Betty's mother, canned the produce. Chickens were raised on the six extra lots Martin bought when he moved the family from Tennessee to be near Minnie's family. The Barnetts also kept Bessie, their milk cow, and cultivated a row of fruit and nut trees on the west edge of the property.

In an interview in her home in DeSoto during the summer of 2011, ninety-four-year-old Betty Barnett Moroni recalled how warm the day had been and how blustery the weather was for that time of the year: "It was a day that shook people's nerves." Heavy rain showers began after she and her nine-year-old sister, Marie, twelve-year-old Tina (pronounced *Tie-nah*) Mae, and their older brother, Herschel, fifteen, walked to the two-story red-brick school across the IC tracks. Built twenty-five years before, it was the tallest building in town.

When they got to the school yard, the Barnett kids separated to join the little collections of friends that made up the all-white student population of 125. DeSoto School had neither running water nor electricity nor a telephone, and the bathroom was a double privy out by the playground's basketball goals. The school was heated with coal warming stoves in each classroom, fed by Uncle Gil, the janitor. He had banked the one in Betty and Marie's room so it was not long before their teacher, Sylvia Bash, asked the boys to open the windows. The first order of the day, as it was every school day, was a recitation of the Pledge of Allegiance to the Flag with hand over heart, followed by bowed heads and the Lord's Prayer.

All morning the winds raced the clouds until it was time for dinner. The school lacked a cafeteria so almost every child walked home to eat, but a few kids from out in the country carried metal dinner pails, just like their fathers took to the mines, and ate at their desks. When the Barnetts reached the IC tracks, sheets of rain dumped from the roiling skies. Minnie stood on the front porch with five-month-old Ruth in her arms. Little six-year-old Elsie Barnett clung to her mother's long skirt. Minnie told Herschel to change into dry clothes but, curiously, directed "the girls to come down to the table in their under-slips." Tina Mae objected. She was beginning to be a woman and was self-conscious about the changes, but Minnie had her way.

During dinner, Minnie walked in from the front parlor with four brand-new Easter dresses she had sewn for her girls at the treadle-powered machine in the front room. The holy day at the Mt. Calvary Evangelical Lutheran church the Barnetts attended was less than a month away. Inexplicably, she asked her girls to wear them back to class. "Tina Mae was always one to

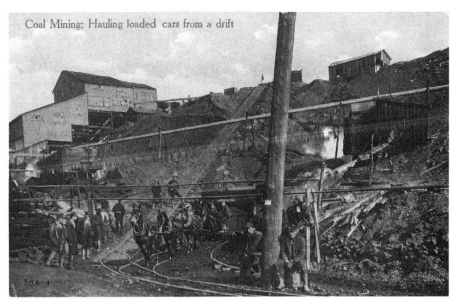

Coal Mining; Hauling loaded cars from a drift

584-4

Team of mules hauling coal from a drift mine. *From an early twentieth-century penny postcard in the author's collection.*

push at the edges," Betty Moroni said. The girl's maternal grandmother had given each of them a dainty gold bracelet for Christmas. Tina Mae wanted to wear the bracelet back to school, but her mother said, "No, the bracelets are for church, besides, we don't want to be showin' no one up now do we, and besides, Gramma would be crushed if you were to lose them." During our interview, Betty, her head cocked to one side, wondered out loud if her mother sensed that something ineffable was afoot. Walking with her sisters and brother back to the DeSoto School, Betty remembered how she "felt pretty for the first time in my life." She had no way of knowing that Tina Mae and Marie and Elsie had less than two hours to live.[8]

In Carterville, out of the direct path of the tornado but still destined to encounter a rolling wall cloud of eighty-mile-an-hour straight-line winds, grade-school teacher Marie South Williams recognized the severity of the storm approaching her school. What she experienced leaves behind a vivid description of the terror impacting the schools, the homes, and the businesses of people all over southern Illinois. "I got under my desk, and the children all got under their seats," she recalled in an interview given in 1984.

> And it got so bad and it commenced to break out some of our windows, why, I asked them to pray. And one little boy, just with a real loud voice, he commenced to pray, "Now I lay me down to sleep."

That's the only prayer I expect he knew. Well, we all just joined in then with his prayer. And we said it all the way through, and we said it twice. And by that time the wind had passed on, and it didn't break any more windows out, and we was up on the second floor in an old brick building. And it seemed like all at once after we had said the second prayer to go to sleep by.

Williams paused for a moment, struggling to control her emotions. "And we all got up out of the—" she stumbled again, "then we said the Lord's Prayer. We was so glad we was all saved. And a lot of them knew the Lord's Prayer. But he didn't start that. He just said, 'Now I lay me down to sleep,' and we went through it twice."[9]

When the Barnett children reached DeSoto School, the wind was blowing a gale out of the southwest. Herschel and his older friends took to tossing their hats into the air to see how far the wind would carry them. The first toss landed Herschel's newsboy hat high in the branches of a tree on the northern perimeter of the muddy playground.

Recess arrived at 2:30 P.M. Out on the playground, the wind was so strong Betty found it difficult to stand and to keep her Easter dress modestly in check so it would not embarrass her. Many children sought shelter in the lee of the school building. Recess usually lasted until 3:00 P.M., but Mr. Sanford, the principal, rang the school bell up in the tower, calling them inside a little early. The central hallway was cave dark. In a loud voice above the building wind, Mr. Sanford said for the children to just go to their classrooms rather than line up by grade as they were accustomed. Mrs. Bash stood at the classroom doorway. She said, "Girls, take your seats. You boys, close the windows."

Outside it was dark as the inside of a nightmare. The wind whistled in the eaves and cuffed the building so hard it shuddered. Window shades went parallel to the floor, vibrating furiously and emitting a high, kazoo whine over the boom of the wind.

And then the Tri-State was upon them.

Windows exploded in the boys' faces.

Girls screamed.

"The wind threw me against the far wall," Betty said. "Something in my side cracked. It hurt so bad," and then the floor, the second floor above her where Tina Mae's and Herschel's classrooms were lifted four feet in the foul air, twisted, then crashed down on Betty's classroom. Hail like oversized mothballs pelted her; one clump the size of an orange similar to what she got every year in her Christmas stocking was beside her in the rubble. Objects suspended inside the vortex whizzed above her head—roofing, whole sides of houses, a mattress, and pieces of lumber.

Betty remembered the screams and the tag ends of prayers lifted to a God who seemed not to care. "I called out to Marie." No answer came. "I saw a window hole close, so I climbed out before the walls collapsed. Everything was gone. DeSoto was flattened for as far as I could see. A horse without a rider galloped by and a milk cow. I was so cold," Betty said, her eyes clos ing for a moment, a hand clenched at the side of her tightened mouth. Her voice faltering noticeably, she said, "My Easter dress was ruined. I wanted so much to ask Momma, did I die?"

"When bodies were taken from the wrecked schoolhouse and laid out, [r]ow after row [of bodies]," the *Post-Dispatch*'s Samuel O'Neil eloquently described. "There was no one to claim the lifeless forms. The children's parents were either dead or on the way to hospitals. The school principal, who escaped death, was called upon to identify the children. His clothes were torn and there were marks on his body to tell of his narrow escape. [H]e was dazed as he stepped from one bundle to another in an effort to identify the dead."[10]

Most accounts of the near aftermath suggested survivors were in shock, numbed by their experience, stunned and unable to process what they now saw. "I may have been rendered temporarily unconscious," Garrett Crews admitted.

> Although I do not know, but at any rate, when I came to myself, I found that I was pinned beneath a wooden beam of some kind and I suspect that I was hysterical, although I don't remember whether I was or not. But I do remember that I was lying on top of our janitor and I could not move. Our janitor's name was Williams and probably his first name of Gilbert because we all called him, Uncle Gil. I was pinned between him and this beam, and he was lying on top of bricks. He attempted to calm me down and said that when he could move some bricks from under himself it would free me from the beam. And that's what he did. . . . Uncle Gil was bald-headed and had a [gash] on his scalp. I was covered with blood but as it turned out, it was all from his wound since I did not have even a scratch on me. I remember scrambling out and over the debris. It is regrettable now when I realize that at the time I apparently gave no thought toward trying to assist any of my schoolmates or teachers.[11]

"Mr. Tippy was walking away from the school," Betty Moroni continued in her living room, a picture of her late husband, Jesse, in permanent residence on the wooden console TV. "Mr. Tippy owned a restaurant. He was holding his son in his arms. So I turned to Mr. Tippy to see if he was real or if I was dead like the rest. I asked him if the world had ended, and he said, 'No,' and he said it was a cyclone. I didn't know what that meant. I was scared and cold and I asked him if he'd see to taking me home. He said I could come with them. We walked to what was left of the businesses along the main road."[12]

Like Herschel, Jane Albon Crews, Garrett's wife, was in a classroom on the second floor of the DeSoto School that day. When the tornado tracked northeast out of town, she found herself "astraddle Irene Forner. I landed in the coal bin. I don't know how I got there. When I got out of school, as Garrett has said, there were all these people yelling, 'Watch out for the hot lines, watch the lines.'"[13] Electric service to DeSoto was less than a year old.

Max Burton worked as an IC Railroad telegraph operator from Tamaroa, Illinois, a whistle stop north of Du Quoin. Upon hearing of what had befallen DeSoto, he jumped in his automobile to be of whatever assistance he could. Blocked by wreckage and debris, of necessity, the final couple of miles were completed on foot. He made it to the school and was appalled that it had become a single story. He, too, reported, "The . . . principal hurried

Remains of the DeSoto business district along Route 2. This is a scene Garrett Crews would have glimpsed on the way home. Saw logs (*foreground*) are ready for loading onto Illinois Central railcars. *From a contemporary postcard in the author's collection.*

DeSoto School and teachers, ca. 1920. The man standing at the far left is presumed to be Mr. Sanford, the principal. The schoolhouse was completed in 1900. *Photo courtesy of the Jackson County Historical Society of Illinois.*

back and forth identifying bodies and helping search for more, even though he staggered. Bleeding from his own injuries and narrow escape, [the principal] was also worrying over the whereabouts and safety of two girl teachers who were unaccounted for. A large crowd struggled in a desperate digging effort, frantic, as the ruins of the building smoldered. Firefighters from nearby towns worked with them, wielding shovels and picks. The fire destroyed what the wind had not."[14] "Childish voices [were] raised in pain and terror filled the air."[15]

According to Max Burton, on the muddy school yard, twenty-five bodies were arrayed on sheets taken down from barkless trees and mattresses collected along the way, but no one had yet come to claim any. Eight more lifeless bodies would be added, one of whom was found in the ruins of the school's privy launched skyward by the ferocious wind with a girl inside to be carried nearly a quarter of a mile over the east-west-running Iron Mountain Railroad tracks. That unfortunate girl was Tina Mae Barnett, discovered two full days after the storm. To this day, Betty agonizes over the chance Tina Mae could have lain injured, alive but helpless, suffering dreadfully before she succumbed to her injuries all alone.

Garrett Crews looked out on the school yard from his second-floor class-room just as the black cloud hit: "[D]own in the northwest corner . . . there was a girls' toilet. And I recall seeing a girl come out of the toilet—the wind picked her up, just head-high or so, and blew her more or less straight north to the fence on the north side of our school building. She was found dead in the fence."[16]

Paul South, sixteen, a classmate of Herschel and Garrett, gave an eyewit-ness account in the *Carbondale Free Press* on March 20, 1925, in which he told of pasting himself to the south wall of the disintegrating school. "It got real dark and I heard a noise like a million trains. The kids all around me started screaming and crying. I prayed but [not] out loud. Then the bricks began to fall. . . . I opened my eyes and saw [kids] being buried beneath the bricks. Some of them had their arms raised as the bricks fell."

South was to run home only to find his house gone, his mother and sister mangled and dead, and his grandmother Mary Heiple seriously hurt. She had been flung underneath a roof from someone else's house. Panicked but under control, he ran to the hard road, State Route 2, and found a Ford Coupe with the keys in it. Appropriating the coupe, South returned to load his grandmother and head south to Carbondale. By this time cars and trucks were streaming north to DeSoto to lend assistance. Debris covering the road

DeSoto business district ruins. This is the scene Betty Barnett Moroni witnessed when she accompanied Mr. Tippy to town. *From the author's postcard collection.*

DeSoto, Illinois, business district. A sign (*far left*) on a door identifies the temporary offices of the Red Cross. *Photo postcard from the author's collection.*

only added to the congestion. The resourceful South was forced to drive a good deal of the way on the IC right-of-way. Grandma Heiple lived to tell the story how the doctors at Holden Hospital believed Paul saved her life. Her face required hundreds of stitches to put her back together, but she lived on. Marie South Williams, Paul's aunt, recounted how she lost two relatives to the winds, Emma Split and Lucille Poulson: "[Em], she was just beat up to pieces. A two-by-four run through her middle."[17]

Those like Mary Heiple who survived a direct hit lived on but with scars both inside and out. Ms. Williams also tells a story about a mother she knew who died, but the babe in her arms lived: "A fire out of the stove must have got coal on the top of the baby's head. And she's never . . . she's living yet and she's never got a hair up there on her head. A piece about like that [*gestures*] and she just combs the whole back of her hair back like that."[18] Her brother lost a son to the storm. He later reported to his sister that someone in Indiana contacted him because he had found a pair of her brother's pants with his Masonic identification card in a soggy pocket, a phenomena not at all uncommon and oft-repeated in the aftermath. Betty Barnett Moroni had a similar experience in her family with a life-insurance policy.

The *St. Louis Post-Dispatch* reported in a front-page story the day after the storm that G. R. Huffman of the Huffman Funeral Home in Carbondale was in DeSoto on business. Recognizing what was about to happen, he leapt from his car, banged on the front door of a bungalow, and then bolted through the door, yelling at the top of his lungs to ask if anyone was home. A scared woman's voice said they were in the living room. A mother and child lay on the floor terrified. Huffman joined them, where they watched as all four walls were torn off the house, the roof disintegrating, but all three survived without injury.

When the tornado arrived, Jesse Pankey was pulling into the garage of his home with his wife and two young children after visiting relatives in Harco, a coal-mining community not far from Harrisburg, Illinois, in Saline County. "Just as he stepped out of the car, the roof of the building was swept away. In an instant his car was lifted into the air, and it sailed away with his wife and children inside. He was airlifted and blown five blocks, falling on the Illinois Central tracks. His wife and children were found in a freshly plowed field, only slightly hurt. The last he saw of his car, it was still sailing through the clouds."[19]

Betty Barnett was escorted by Mr. Tippy's brother to a large home where the injured were gathering, trying to unite with family. Ruth, Elsie, her father, Martin, and her mother, Minnie, arrived at late dusk with the fires backlighting their tearful reunion. Unhurt because he had had the quickness of mind to seek shelter under his desk as the teachers screamed at their students to save themselves, Herschel was still working at the school. Minnie told Betty her sister Marie was dead, that Herschel had helped excavate her lifeless body, and that Tina Mae was missing. Martin's head was swathed in a dirty, blood-soaked sheet. He was not right, Betty could tell, and never would be even to his own admission. Little Elsie was in Minnie's arms, unmoving, a great bruise on her head. Elsie was muddy and unconscious. Ruth and Minnie had been out in the yard. Minnie had just enough time to snatch her daughter away from the wind before they were levitated and blown into a treetop. Neither was hurt but for scratches. The family wandered into the business area. Rumors suggested medical help could be found there, but the rumors were untrue. No doctors were coming to DeSoto.

On Thursday, the *Carbondale Free Press* told readers, "A truck load of bodies arrived at Du Quoin from DeSoto an hour or so before the relief special [an IC train] reached Du Quoin while to Carbondale were brought the bodies of the little tots from six to ten years who perished when the school house collapsed." One of those children was Marie Barnett. She was buried in the rubble of bricks, mortar, and timbers. The IC backed a train of baggage cars from Carbondale to DeSoto, the bodies laid neatly on the wooden floors and then taken to the National Guard Armory.

South façade of the DeSoto schoolhouse ruins where thirty-three children died. The structure has been reduced to a half story. *Photo courtesy of the West Franklin (Illinois) Historical District and Silkwood Inn Museum.*

By midnight the first night, 20 percent of the population would be counted dead or injured and taken to the appropriate sites in Carbondale and Du Quoin, but that statistic can be somewhat misleading because most of the men in DeSoto were away working in the mines. Had the storm raced through on the weekend, the death toll would have been substantially higher. Most of the men who died were older and unable to work away from the home.

At 3 P.M. on Thursday, an IC train left Centralia with three empty refrigerator cars, "stopped in DeSoto and filled the cars with bodies."[20] That same day, a man in a suit with a megaphone to his mouth stood outside the DeSoto Red Cross headquarters hastily billeted in a badly damaged business on Route 2, asking for help in the identification of a baby taken the night before to Herrin Hospital. "Every few moments someone who has just arrived rushes in [to the office] for information," a newspaper reported.[21]

Scott Field sent medical staff commanded by post commandant Colonel Paegelow to Du Quoin. Airmen at the dirigible base attempted to make contact with the area by short-wave radio. Command wanted to dispatch airships, but it was decided the "atmospheric conditions" would prevent them from reaching the area. The next two days air corps biplanes flew from town to town delivering supplies and "rescue apparatus."[22] For many southern Illinoisans, the planes were the first they had ever seen.

The DeSoto dead, mostly children, were laid in rows on the floor of Carbondale's National Guard Armory. When Holden Hospital was filled with casualties, a facility operating with a new $150,000 addition managed by the Methodist Church and the Woman's Home Missionary Society, the Elks Club on West Jackson Street was put into service. Parents, children, and grandparents searching for missing loved ones arrived to claim their dead. Many of the corpses were naked or only partially draped with a soiled sheet or robe filched off a tree, or the bodies were burned as though they had emerged from the Devil's pyres. "Plaster from the walls and ceiling of the school had been ground into [the children's] faces."[23]

"As a gray-haired woman tottered by a row of bodies of school children . . . tears streaming down her cheeks, she turned to a companion and sobbed, 'This is NO disaster, it is a crucifixion!'"[24] Many people were so overcome they fainted or became hysterical and had to be physically restrained.

By the late afternoon, a "stream of automobiles was moving to Du Quoin fourteen miles north, from an early hour to well past midnight. The state Highway . . . was alive with automobiles which tourists readily offered to take injured and dying to the hospitals at Du Quoin and Carbondale. All other traffic was held up by officers to give the right-of-way to the cars of mercy. This traffic grew until there was a line of standing automobiles six miles in length. The license plates on these cars proved they were from many states."[25]

This was Betty Barnett's recollection, too. When her battered family reached the business district, cars were lined up on Route 2.[26] A man from Carbondale drove them north to Du Quoin in his sedan, its side curtains in place against the chill. The family was dropped off at Marshall Browning Hospital. Betty would never see Elsie alive again. Martin was immediately taken upstairs where the wards were while Minnie, Ruth, and Betty were relegated to the basement.

Somewhere in the troubled night, Betty awoke to her mother's gentle shaking. A nurse from a race of titans so tall she blocked the single-bulb light in the ceiling hulked over them.

> Momma, she said for me to go with the nurse. But I just scrunched into her side, Momma's smell a comfort to me. Momma said the nurse needed my help, that this would be the brave thing to do. We stood up together. The nurse bent down so's her eyes were at my level. Blood was on her white uniform. She said, "We need your help to

identify someone about your age, see if you know his name, 'cause we can't get nothin' from him. His people need to know he's alright." That nurse smiled, then. I remember nodding and walking up the stairs. Everything was painted gray. People lying on beds with wheels lined the halls, some were moaning, and crying, I heard a real loud shriek. I thought this had to be what our preacher called Hell. We came to the end of a corridor that must have been a mile long and stopped. This time, the giant nurse kneeled in front of me and said she was going to open the extra-wide door and wanted me to take a look at someone for her. She did and when that door was part the way open, someone inside began to wail in the loudest most scared voice I ever heard. Standing straight up in the bed, I knew him as soon as I laid eyes on him even though he was all cut up and dirty, his clothes, rags. He was screaming over and over, "No! No-o! Leave me be! I don't want to go like Momma done! No-o! Go away!" I told the giant who he was and ran to Momma. I've kept his name secret all these years. No need for folks to know.

Betty spent the night in clean sheets in a kind stranger's home in Du Quoin and the following day was picked up by Minnie's relatives and taken to live with them in Hurst, Illinois.

The generosity of Americans is without peer and abundantly illustrated in the storm's aftermath. Several sources witnessed the women of DeSoto taking up a collection along the line of automobiles attracted to the scene. Some said they raised several thousand dollars, which they handed over to the Red Cross.

DeSoto turned to burying its dead. Officials were anxious to inter as quickly as possible to eliminate the possibility of disease. Sixty-five men from surrounding towns reported to the National Guard to help dig graves.

Saturday, thirty victims were buried at the DeSoto Cemetery in a mass grave, but only a handful of people attended. Most of those who would normally be present were either dead or incapacitated and in the hospital. Among those buried were six members of the Ebersoll family, five from the Farmer family, and a mystery man named Musical Dan (see appendix). Hearses arriving from surrounding towns disgorged caskets, black for mothers and fathers and gray for children. A reporter for the Associated Press wrote, "Before noon the little town, deserted except for DeSoto people, began receiving back its own. A hearse from Carbondale would enter the cemetery, unload its burden and hurry away." A biplane circled the "cemetery three times, dipping gracefully as it swung over the open graves."[27]

One of those interred was Elsie Barnett, who died of head injuries in Herrin hospital on the twenty-second. That sad morning Tina Mae and Marie were laid to rest, too. Side-by-side-by-side the sisters yet lie together. The pain in her eyes obvious, Betty recounted that Elsie had been clothed in a green dress Betty had never seen before.

Betty said that in the spring of 1926, "Poppa was hauling a load of coal during mud season when he stood up in the seat to ask a question of a man walking along the street, he asked him, 'Hey Mister, do ya think this team can pull me through that puddle? I'm not feelin' real good.' Poppa, he fell over onto the muddy street dead. Momma thought he'd had a heart attack but I think it was because of a broken heart he died."[28]

Minnie Barnett was three months' pregnant, carrying Betty's new brother, Martin. She had four hungry children to feed and clothe near the onset of the Great Depression.

> Pitiful were the stories of the burials. . . . As the burials proceeded, children no longer awed by the scene . . . began playing about the tombstones and clambering on the rough wooden boxes piled beside the . . . graves. Neighbors would read the penciled names on the wooden box[es], affix the name to a cross or temporary headstone and carry it to the grave. Boxes of flowers sent from Chicago . . . were sorted into 71 small sprays by women who explained, "We have no flowers and we do not want to miss anyone."[29]

A reporter for the *Carbondale Free Press* was inspired to paint this poignant picture: "There were a few women with tear stained faces, a few tots who sobbed constantly, and a few men, most of the latter returning to dig graves between intermittent funerals. Under gray skies the little knots of men and women gathered early in the morning in the little cemetery marked here and there by a few imposing monuments, but for the most part dotted by wooden markers, some of them [memorialized] with a fruit jar filled with . . . flowers."[30]

4

West Frankfort, Illinois

t 2:53 P.M., five miles northeast of DeSoto, the storm reached Bush, a mining camp of flimsy, cookie-cutter, unpainted frame homes lining the dirt streets in rows. The community boasted a company store, a dance hall, a skating rink, dentists and doctors, a soda fountain/sweet shop, a US Post Office, and a two-story building that served as mining headquarters. In less than a minute, seven people died, and thirty-seven were injured. Still running along the ground a hot sixty-plus miles an hour, still a lethal F5, and three-quarters of a mile in width, the high winds tracked over open farm country for fourteen miles through Williamson and Franklin Counties. Twenty-four more southern Illinoisans died.

Rebuilt miners' homes in Bush, ca. 1939. Photo by Arthur Rothstein. *From Herbert Russell*, A Southern Illinois Album: Farm Security Administration Photographs, 1936–1943 *(Carbondale: Southern Illinois University Press, 1990), 41.*

New Orient Mine No. 2, West Frankfort. The elevated rail bed to the left is referred to as the "hump track." Early twentieth-century penny postcard. *From the author's collection.*

In Franklin County's Six Mile Township, an iron bridge lost one complete span and was rendered useless. At the Big Muddy River in the county's southeast corner, the winds overwhelmed an eighth-mile-long IC Railroad bridge shoving it several feet off its sturdy concrete foundation.

Next was the largest town in the storm track, West Frankfort, Illinois. With a population of nearly eighteen thousand, this was Egypt's biggest city, and it enjoyed a thriving economy based on coal mining and industries that supported it. Two of the largest coal mines in the United States, New Orient No. 2, owned by the Chicago, Williamson, and Franklin Coal Company, based in Chicago, and Old Ben No. 8, were within the city limits.

Now a mile wide, the roiling, black wall first struck southwest West Frankfort at Joiner School a little after 3:00 P.M., the end of second shift in the mines. "All morning, before the tornado, it had rained. The day was dark and gloomy; the air heavy. Then the drizzle increased," said one witness. "The heavens seemed to open, pouring down a flood. The day grew black.

"Then the air was filled with 10,000 things. Boards, poles, cans, garments, stoves, whole sides of . . . houses. In some cases the houses themselves were picked up and smashed to earth. And living beings, too."[1]

The tornado hit the New Addition, the local nickname for the almost two-year-old neighborhood close to New Orient No. 2, situated in the northwest part of town, where the storm did its worst damage. Most of the miners here owned their small, clapboarded homes like those at Bush, because the strength of the United Mine Workers Union, the dominant political force in West Frankfort, prevented coal companies from forcing their workers to live in captivity in company-store towns like Zeigler. Accounts vary as to the number of homes destroyed from 250 to more than 500.

To the eight hundred miners toiling five hundred feet underground at New Orient No. 2, the first sign something was amiss was when the electric lights flickered and then went out. Ventilation fans and sump pumps stopped operating. The hoist that carried both miners and coal in the main shaft went quiet, and at least for a few moments, the men must have thought they had been buried alive by a cave-in. Their bottom boss ordered them to fire the carbide lights on their obligatory hard hats, just as they had been trained. The men formed a single-file line to evacuate. Twenty-six years later, on the cusp of the official Christmas vacation, New Orient No. 2, notorious for an abundance of methane, would experience an explosion on December 21 that would kill 119 miners, the fourth ugliest toll in US history, but this day in 1925, the miners were spared hardship until they reached the top of the zigzag, metal escape ladders.

Remains of New Addition, where miners and their families lived in frame houses. This is what confronted the miners when they exited Orient No. 2. A team of horses drags away what looks to be a roof. Photo was snapped from the hump tracks above the New Orient No. 2 Mine, West Frankfort. *Photo courtesy of the West Franklin (Illinois) Historical District and Silkwood Inn Museum.*

What ran through these tough men's minds as they ascended? What anxieties? Had news of the storm slowly filtered down to them by word of mouth? Did they merely think that power had been lost as it had so many times before? Whatever the miners thought, whatever personal preconceptions might have been formed, few could have imagined what waited on the surface. Not a single man escaped without the loss of someone dear or uninsured property or all he had worked for to that point in his life.

The damage was every bit as horrifying as that at Gorham, Murphysboro, and DeSoto. Tough miners, many World War I vets, their faces blackened by coal dust after working most of second shift, tears guttering white channels in the coal dust, raced along muddy streets strewn with the fresh wreckage of their lives. "The air was full of cries and screams," the Alton, Illinois, paper reported.[2] Many miners ran to the high school to check on their teenagers. To their relief, the school was undamaged. Joiner School on the southwest outskirts lost windows and a section of roof; yet, the children were safe. Not so fortunate were two frame schools recently built to absorb the mine-sponsored population growth in the city. The schoolhouse used for first grade collapsed on the pupils. Charles Church's stepdaughter died. The schoolhouse for second grade spun off its foundation but remained intact with few injuries to those persons in it.[3]

The March 19 *West Frankfort Daily American* reported that a "ragged little girl comes near, crying for her momma. No one could answer her questions. A miner, still in his pit clothes, comes toward the crowd, his tall, thin body in striking contrast to the pitiful, bloody bundle which he held limp in his arms. The bundle was five year old Leroy ROBERTS" (see appendix).

Because the tornado had ripped out telegraph and telephone lines, the first inkling in Benton, six miles to the north, that something was terribly wrong with their neighbor came with a messenger who drove to the Benton fire station to ask for help putting out the fires. Soon, State Route 37 was clogged with sightseers, those who wanted to help, and relatives and friends seeking firsthand information on their people.[4] Delivery trucks in West Frankfort were pressed into service as ambulances, as were dozens of autos.

In New Addition, bodies were covered with mud because the streets were not paved.

Becky Reed, the infant daughter of a frantic West Frankfort miner, was missing, and so was his wife until a searcher saw a baby's booty sticking out from the pile of boards that remained of the Reed home. The searcher pulled gently, and Becky Reed emerged. "She was unhurt," a reporter wrote, but one has to wonder just who was "Infant of C. P. Reed" in the official casualty list (see appendix).[5]

New Addition, West Frankfort. *Photo courtesy of the West Franklin (Illinois) Historical District and Silkwood Inn Museum.*

Another paper reported, "A five day old infant squalling in a perambulator was pulled safely from a pile of kindling that had been a home," and mere feet away, the infant's mother lay mutilated.[6]

A laborer by trade, Charles Biggs was driving into West Frankfort from the west just as the tornado hit. His car threatening to roll over from the blunt force of the wind, he jumped from his vehicle, only to see it roll away, a mere plaything to the wind. Through streets where bedlam reigned, he raced toward home but must have realized very quickly that the closer he approached, the more thoroughly his neighbors' homes were either damaged or completely erased. "I found my daughter-in-law sitting up dazed," he said, "and she died whilst I tried to talk with her. Her two daughters were twenty-five feet away, dead. My wife and mother were there, too, dead. Nearby was my twenty-one year old son, Fred. He was dead and near him was my daughter, Margaret. She was sixteen two days ago, and she was dead. My other daughter at school was the only one saved. I was only scratched."[7] One wonders if he felt guilty for having survived. Did he possess the will to go on after losing seven of the eight people in his family?

Eyewitnesses gave testament to the awful carnage. One of them was a traveling man, Jacob L. Wolf of Denver, Colorado, in town calling on storeowners, selling them on stocking his top-drawer line of dry goods. He told the *St. Louis Post-Dispatch* he saw an elderly woman levitated by the wind and sailed at least three hundred feet down the street only to fall to her death a twisted bundle. The newspaper on March 19 reported, "Near the roundhouse of the Chicago and Eastern Illinois Railroad was found the body of a man, his neck broken while a 2 × 4 had pierced the lower portion of his body. Another woman was found with a stick driven though her head." Later on that night, "an unusual stillness" came upon the torn city, a silence interrupted only by sirens.

Since the majority of the men in town were underground at the time of the tornado, as was the case in DeSoto, most of the injured were mothers and their children. Of the 148 who died, 40 percent were children; 410 people were injured, and over 2,000 became homeless. In the immediate area, fifteen hundred miners were below ground, yet only one fatality was reported, a man who failed to find shelter in the above-ground vaults ubiquitous to businesses of the day to secure payroll cash.

Casualties were transported by whatever means available to the United Mine Worker's Hospital, a building lucky to survive with its position mere blocks from the Tri-State's track. Churches opened their doors as did individuals to house the homeless and the hurt. A relief train from St. Louis showed up near midnight with doctors and medical supplies, but finding little to do there, personnel dispersed into the countryside to do what good they could. Because a local chapter of the Salvation Army maintained offices in West Frankfort, relief was quicker here than in other towns in the storm track. By Thursday morning, the delivered medical supplies, blankets, cots, foodstuffs, and tents were already being put to good use.

Company K from the Cairo armory, under the command of Captain L. E. Hall, and Company L from Salem rushed by train to West Frankfort. The military commandeered six buildings on South Emma Street. By Thursday afternoon the militia secured all entrances to the city to prevent looting as well as keep only authorized workers on the scene. "There was no red tape; there was no waiting for invitations. The Army came and did its bit," was the terse description of *St. Louis Post-Dispatch* newsman Arthur H. Schneff in a March 22, 1925, story.

Martial law was not declared, but several reporters complained about the tightness of the cordon. Only those privileged autos with signs in their windshields attesting to the fact the driver or rider was a "DOCTOR" or "OFFICERS" or "RED CROSS" were allowed through the armed roadblocks. The use of restored telegraph services at railroad facilities was reserved for emergency purposes, forcing newspapermen to travel as far as Mt. Vernon— thirty miles north—over congested roads, some of which were unpaved and muddy tracks, to call stories in to their editors. Others gave up in frustration and returned to their home offices.

Three days after the tornado, chaos still ruled, as the front page of the March 22 *St. Louis Post-Dispatch* observed.

On the streets of the city, strangely silent crowds shifted about. Ambulances shot back and forth with noisy bells. The congestion of the wounded in their resting places, and activities of willing volunteers increased the confusion. Girls who probably never saw serious wounds before gave what help they could.

There was no great outcry from the sufferers. Here and there one moaned in agony. Faces above makeshift covers strove to repress the signs of pain and sorrow and fear. Men with fractured skulls lay quiet. Strangers comforted children with broken limbs. Maimed women sought news of their babies. Youths who could move a bit begged cigarettes. Those who needed operations but had to wait their turn submitted gladly to opiates as physicians reached them. Everywhere the glare of electric lights and the stir of people kept the wounded awake.

Before midnight eighty-four of West Frankfort's dead had reached the morgues and embalmers struggling against time in cramped rooms amid interruptions by crowds of anxious survivors seeking relatives. Some bodies bore livid mutilations or burns. Formaldehyde fumes assailed the eyes. Worst sight of all, and one which turned everyone away with a gulp, was a row of sixteen dead children of tender years huddled on a table. One mother was lying in bed . . . her breast torn open and a tiny infant crawling around her cold body attempting to nurse.

Another eyewitness said of the same scene,

Skulls crushed, backs broken, faces and bodies bruised, and cut almost beyond recognition, the silent figures await identification. Passing on through the grisly room [lit by coal oil lamps,] one comes upon a dozen undertakers working busily through the night washing the cold forms, embalming them and laying them away to await claim. Then, on into the outer shed where men and women are corded down two long rows of casket boxes, draped in blankets and quilts awaiting their turn in the work room.[8]

The punishing task of sorting victims went deep into the night. Groups of refugees huddled around campfires fueled by abundant wooden debris.

Salvation Army's West Frankfort offices, from which invaluable service was given to the homeless, the hungry, and the bereaved. *Photo postcard from the author's collection.*

Where cries were heard from the wreckage, men did what they could for rescue. A call went out from campfire to campfire that officers of the United Mine Workers asked for grave diggers to report to the union hall at first light.

The dead were conveyed by whatever means available to temporary morgues in church basements and fraternal lodges just as they had been in Murphysboro. Doors torn from their hinges, 2 × 4s with bedspreads tied off between them, two pairs of strong hands and backs, all were pressed into service as stretchers to deliver the injured. When Union Hospital reached capacity, overflows were driven to Benton's five-year-old Moore Hospital, located in the Wood Building on the public square's north side. Herrin Hospital, thirteen miles southwest, was pressed into service also, just as it had been with casualties from DeSoto and Bush. West Frankfort's city hall became a triage center.

Within days, the city received 200 tents, 11,000 tent stakes, 599 cots, 148 stoves, 543 pillows, 580 bed sacks, and 888 stove joints. Five days after the Tri-State Tornado, the Salvation Army was serving three thousand meals a day.[9]

The tornado lopped off the northwest quadrant of the city. However, most West Frankfort residents were largely unaware of the severity of the damage.

Unlike Murphysboro and DeSoto, West Frankfort's waterworks was operational, so fires were doused, saving the city from the all-consuming conflagrations of its demolished neighbors, yet the demand for water to fight fires was so extreme, the municipal supply was soon exhausted. In a message sent by railroad telegraph, the National Guard made arrangements for rail tank cars to deliver potable water from Herrin. Survivors also used existing onsite wells and rainwater cisterns.

Six miles west of West Frankfort, the coal-mining town of Zeigler felt fortunate because it escaped the storm. When news of its neighbor's demise reached the community late in the afternoon, townspeople gathered in the Zeigler Circle, on a slight prominence in the town center. Here, an impressive mine headquarters, now razed, had been built by Harvard-educated Joseph Leiter, who, on occasion, wearing a custom-tailored red topcoat with tails, rode to work in an open carriage drawn by a pair of white horses in the command of a black footman in formal livery.

"The horizon was blushed with flames of burning cities which were in the path of the storm," the *Zeigler News* said on March 20. "From Desoto [*sic*] comes the report of a city burning. In the east the sky was ablaze from the fires at West Frankfort, and to the west the flames of Murphysboro twenty miles away were seen leaping into the sky."

Richard Baumhoff, *St. Louis Post-Dispatch* staff correspondent, witnessed the same angry flare in the eastern sky as he neared West Frankfort on an emergency train. His fear West Frankfort was conflagrated like DeSoto and Murphysboro was allayed when he learned that a previously smoldering gob pile had been fanned by the winds into a considerable blaze, not the city.

Pathos was abundant in West Frankfort, but few reports match that of "a dirty ragged man with bandaged head [who] staggered into [the] office" of the West Frankfort relief center. James Williams, thirty-six years old, proceeded to tell the story of how he was sitting on his front porch enjoying the balmy day near New Orient Mine and watching the storm come up when first thing he knew, something hit him, "'and I rolled away, got up, got smacked down and rolled again. The house blew away and they found my wife and baby dead. I tried to help rescue others as long as I could, [but, you see] I fell asleep in a tailor shop downstairs today till they closed it. For God's sake,' he groaned. 'Give me a place to sleep.'"[10]

Thursday morning dawned cold and clear, and many, many citizens were still unaccounted for. A swampy area north of town was suspected as the depository. Resting with a broken arm in a sling in the improvised City Hall hospital, a three-year-old boy remained unclaimed. He had been found wandering the outskirts of West Frankfort. "Attendants were unable to understand the lad when he tried to tell them his name, but he is sure his parents will call for him. Nurses have not told him . . . there are several 'unknowns' in the adult section of the local morgue," the March 24 *Benton Evening News* reported.

Looting was prevalent. In West Frankfort a policeman shot dead on the spot a man who was attempting to steal the gold wedding band from a dead woman's finger. The April 4 *West Frankfort Daily American* also contained this warning: "Women and girls are asked to stay off the streets . . . by city and county officials due to men of all character swarming into the city since the tornado. These are men of character such that they have no respect for women."

One week after the storm, the *Benton Evening News* reported, "Plundering, pilfering, and thievery have broken out in West Frankfort according to advisors from the police department there this morning." Conditions were so lawless that a citizen's committee petitioned the National Guard to remain in West Frankfort. In response, the mayor and chief of police were trying to devise a workable plan to ensure the safety of the victims.[11]

East of West Frankfort, in the mining village of Caldwell, St. Louis–domiciled Peabody Coal Company ran mine No. 18, which employed five hundred workers, most of them from West Frankfort. They were working over five hundred feet below the surface and a mile and a half back from the main shaft when the Tri-State Tornado ran over the top.

When the tornado arrived, John Knight and Charles Sinks, both weighmen, were working at the top of No. 18's tipple, a derrick-like, metal structure that raises both men and coal in the vertical shaft that leads to the coal seam. The weighmen had quite a ride. Looking like the broken neck of an incredibly tall giraffe, the tipple toppled to the ground. Knight walked away, but Sinks broke both legs. Jack Burbage and Edward Joicey of Smith

New Addition, West Frankfort. *From a contemporary postcard; courtesy of the Frankfort Area Historical Museum.*

Remains of Peabody Mine No. 18, Caldwell, Illinois. *Photo courtesy of the Frankfort Area Historical Museum.*

Street, Benton, were in the washhouse at No. 18. It blew down around them. "Buried in bricks and mortar [Burbage] dug himself out without injury," the March 20 *West Frankfort Daily American* reported, but Joicey had internal injuries and several broken ribs. He said in a car on the way to the United Mine Worker's Hospital, West Frankfort, that he saw two small children walk into the washhouse ahead of the tornado but because of his injuries was unable to dig for them. What happened to the children remains a mystery.

Seventy-five miners' cars parked at No. 18 were demolished; some tumbled as far away as a hundred yards. And at the rural Neal School on Four Mile Lane east of Caldwell, a student, Easter Summers, noticed the tornado sucked every drop of water from the well in the schoolyard.[12]

Seven members of the Uncle Ike Karnes family in and around Eighteen, as Caldwell itself was sometimes called, died that day. For years Ike had kept a general store in Caldwell. During the funerals, ranks of coffins holding the Karnes dead dominated one whole wall of the sanctuary of the country church in which the family had worshipped for decades. So many mourners attended the memorial service that windows and doors were thrown open so the gathered could hear the comforting words of the preacher assuring them the promise of a peaceful eternity in heaven was real.

After the tornado, speculation about reasons for Egypt's desolation and extreme loss of life were discussed anywhere people gathered. Some laid the blame on the region's lawless reputation, rationalizing that Egypt was

Chesapeake, Baltimore, and Ohio railcar blown from the hump track at Orient No. 2, crushing five Tin Lizzies. *Photo courtesy of the West Franklin (Illinois) Historical District and Silkwood Inn Museum.*

a lightning rod for divine retribution intended to clean up the gun battles in the streets, killing of striking miners, lynching of blacks, bootlegging rackets, and gambling. One of the speculators was the Reverend Robert Hall of the First Center of Practical Christianity based in St. Louis. He preached that the tornado's destruction was a "result of the hatred and violence in that part of the country." He went further by specifically blaming the tragedy on the Ku Klux Klan, explaining that their leader in Egypt—S. Glenn Young in Herrin—was especially targeted when he was the first person to die, although the reverend never enlightened the congregation with a name or time of death.[13] Young actually died in a shootout on January 24, 1925, at the European Hotel in downtown Herrin, two months before the tornado. His assailant was a bootlegger lawman by the name of Ora Thomas, who was affiliated with the Egypt-based Charlie Birger and Shelton gangs, both of which supplied the towns in the track of the Tri-State with bootleg hooch. Fifteen thousand people turned out for Young's funeral procession, which featured five mounted Klansmen in full night-rider gear of hoods and robes with bedsheet caparisons for their horses.

Eight-year-old Vernon Dotson of Deering, Illinois, lived just three miles northeast of West Frankfort and was home from school when the Tri-State struck. Creating a scene straight out a horror movie, the woman who sheltered his family unsettled his siblings as she paced the floor for hours looping, "It's gonna turn 'round and come back, you'll see; it's gonna turn right 'round and come back."[14]

5

Parrish and Crossville, Illinois;
Griffin, Owensville, and Princeton, Indiana;
Dissipation

PARRISH, ILLINOIS

Just before 3:15 P.M., the tornado tracked northeast of West Frankfort into
lightly populated agricultural country in rural Franklin County, a period
in the tornado's history representing a quarter of the total storm's path.
The tiny farming community with the ironic name of Parrish was leveled
by F5 winds. In less than two minutes, twenty-two townspeople died, and
another sixty were injured, giving Parrish a casualty rate of 27 percent. With
"[j]ust over half of its long journey completed," wrote Drake University me-
teorologist Wallace Akin, in his 2002 book, *The Forgotten Storm*, "already
it left behind 554 dead and 1,426 injured."[1] Akin, a Fulbright scholar who
was born in 1923 and grew up in Murphysboro, was securely in his mother's
arms when the Tri-State Tornado picked up their home, plucked the roof
off, spun it around, and set it back down with no injury to either of them.
Family stories kindled his lifelong interest in weather.

A crossroads town of about 250, Parrish was connected to the world
by an IC Railroad spur. Forty buildings filled the modest grid of streets,
including a post office, two stores, a restaurant, two garages, and a church.
After the storm moved on, little was left without damage or total ruin.
Nearly all of the residents at home that horrid Wednesday were killed or
injured. Parrish's infrastructure annihilated, funerals had to be held in
adjacent towns.

If they did not operate a business in town, Parrish men worked at nearby Logan in the Black Star Mine, a unionized underground operation owned by the John A. Logan Coal Company.

Much like DeSoto, Bush, and, to a lesser extent, Murphysboro, the majority of the Parrish dead were women and children. Arthur Schneff of the *Post-Dispatch* observed, "From [Logan] to Parrish—and beyond—is a continual panorama of destruction. The road is lined with pieces of furniture, wagon wheels, clothing, bits of torn curtains and bedding, metal bedposts, dead fowls, pieces of timber, and parts of wrecked houses."[2] For mile upon mile, dead or severely injured cows, chickens, horses, and hogs littered the muddy fields, and some of the surviving animals huddled together in what had been their barnyard. The barn erased, its vegetation-free outline became a ghost in a littered debris field.

Clem Launius and his wife, Isabelle, owned a house in the southwest part of Parrish. Four family members were living in the modest home when Clem left early that fateful morning to work at the Black Star Mine. His shift over at 4 P.M., Clem left the mine, oblivious to the horrors that awaited him. As he normally did, Clem walked the two miles home along the IC right-of-way. The closer he grew, the worse the destruction became. He began to run when he caught first sight of what remained of his town. Nothing was standing. Parrish no longer existed. Poppy, one of Clem's friends, stopped him by the arm, and it was then that Poppy told Clem that Isabelle was dead. Poppy led him to where the inert and maimed body lay three hundred feet from home. Overcome with grief, Clem knelt, lifted Isabelle from the mud, and carried her to where their lives used to be lived. Clem's other family members were not killed.[3]

Seeing the black cloud approaching just as school was to let out for the day, Principal Delmar Perryman, like Principal J. E. Fischer in Murphysboro, made a critical decision. He locked the doors on the fifty students who were eager to head home. By the time the winds calmed and hail the size of lemons had fallen, Parrish was reduced to one house, the Primitive Methodist Church, and, paradoxically, Parrish School.

The 3:30 P.M. IC evening train pulled into where the depot had just been. Onboard, returning home from a shopping trip to Eldorado twenty-five miles southeast, were Mrs. Ivory Williams and her two children, the family of Parrish's station agent and postmaster. "The first thing she saw when she alighted was the body of her husband lying among the fallen wires of a telegraph pole, crushed and burned. He died a few hours later in Benton."[4]

All means of communicating the tragedy at Parrish compromised, the engineer backed the train the three miles to Thompsonville, immediately east of West Frankfort, to broadcast the disaster at Parrish and to rally relief efforts. Purely by chance, Dr. J. J. Pennington, a physician from Cedar Rapids, Iowa, on his way to Paducah, Kentucky, was waiting for a rail connection. Responding to the enormity of the funnel cloud he had witnessed, the doctor commandeered all the surgical dressings and antiseptic solutions he could find in Thompsonville and awaited transportation to what he assumed would be a wasteland. Upon arrival in Parrish, he organized relief workers and was instrumental in triaging victims, stabilizing their injuries as quickly as possible, and carrying them on the train to Benton for hospitalization. "The train had several flatcars and a caboose. . . . [M]any of the injured were put in the caboose, and . . . the dead . . . on one of the flatcars," and the rest of Parrish rode the reserve flatcars.[5]

On that train of mercy was the Parks family, who became the centerpiece in an unearthly story the *Benton Evening News* articulated that clearly illustrates just how fickle the ferocious winds of a tornado can be. "Little Margaret [Parks], who is a guest at the home of the writer, earnestly tells of the things she saw," wrote the reporter for the March 20 *Evening News*.

> "The sky was dark, and the wind commenced blowing, oh so hard," she says. "We were scared and before we knew it we were blown away and our home was ruined. When I woke up Mother was holding me tight in her arms and we were way out in the field. A great plank was on me and my dress was gone, a nail or something had torn my underwear. Daddy picked us up and we went to Parrish and then they brought us over here [Benton, Illinois] on the train." Margaret's father explained that he and his family were carried on the wind a quarter of a mile from home. "I did not remember anything after the storm struck until I found myself holding a fencepost," Mr. Parks said. "I happened to glance over my shoulder and saw my little boy in the air, only a few feet above the ground and coming directly toward me. I reached and was barely able to grasp him by the leg."

A cloudless night too quickly followed the storm. Fires flickered in Parrish, but they afforded insufficient light to see the grim situation the town had become. Families able to leave packed what they could find of their belongings onto horse-drawn wagons and sought refuge with friends or relatives. Most would never return. At sunup, family members struggled back to town looking for missing loved ones. "A family, searching near Parrish for their father, found his body in a clump of trees at least a quarter of a mile from his house, his legs and neck broken, his right arm missing, and with a severe wound to the head."[6]

Parrish never rebuilt and today exists as a rural zip code with a smattering of widely dispersed houses.

HAMILTON COUNTY, ILLINOIS

Between 3:30 and 4:00 P.M., still running with a forward speed of sixty miles an hour, the tornado raced northeast on the same track initiated in the Ozark uplands of southeast Missouri two and a half hours earlier. The tornado bisected Hamilton County and its rolling, densely planted farmland and then churned the rich lowlands of the Wabash River floodplain in White County. Hamilton County's seat, McLeansboro, and White's, Carmi, were spared. One should not intimate that the tornado was losing strength, for this was not the case. Casualty counts slowed simply because very few people called these rural counties home. Even so, Hamilton and White Counties suffered 65 dead and 140 injured.

Hamilton County enjoyed a peak population of more than twenty thousand citizens in 1900 but after that bled population rapidly. When the Tri-State Tornado crossed the county, population had swooned to about 14,500. Population density was a scant thirty-three people per square mile, with one-third living in the county seat of Carmi. In the rural areas, which make up most of the county's land space, population density was twenty-eight people per square mile. Even so, thirty-three died in the rubble of their farms. The Ballards and Smiths lost four family members apiece that afternoon.

In southeast Hamilton County near Braden on Greasy Creek, Lonnie and Lillie Smith's house was in the middle of the tornado's track. Despite a storm cellar out back for such emergencies, for whatever reason, a tragic decision was made for the family to ride it out inside their farmhouse. Perhaps the approaching storm caught them by surprise or someone did not want to get drenched. No one will ever know. But what is known is they did not stand a chance. The house and barn flew north in pieces creating a debris field of the Smith family's life that deposited on a hillside as far away as Chicago's Willis Tower is tall. As though no more substantial than ragdolls, the Smiths were sucked into the spinning vortex. Belva, seventeen, sailed into a treetop one-and-a-half football fields away, her lifeless body wrapped around the trunk. Lonnie, Lillie, and their twenty-one-year-old son, Roy, were indecorously dumped from great height into a neighbor's hog lot. When the bodies were discovered, the hogs were feeding on them. Every bristle on the hogs' bodies had been stripped by the wind.[7]

Scant remains of what was once the farmhouse of John Lampley of Macedonia, Illinois, not far from Hogg Creek. John, sixty-five, died during the storm, and his wife, Mary, was injured. *From a contemporary postcard by Hungate Photo; image courtesy of the Hamilton County (Illinois) Historical Society.*

Lawrence Smith told a story about how he, too, was picked up by the wind. While airborne for a distance he could not estimate, a cow rose up to meet him. Smith tried to grab hold of the animal but was unsuccessful.

Parker's Prairie School and Braden Valley, Olga, and Hoodsville Schools were all destroyed. Survivors trucked the dead and injured to McLeansboro, where the ostentatious brick mansion of Mary E. C. McCoy—heir to a local banking fortune—was put to use as a field hospital at the insistence of the Red Cross. Built in 1884, the interior was designed with many large rooms and spacious hallways, making it ideal for its role in helping the community. Mrs. McCoy bequeathed the mansion to the city for use as a library to which purpose it serves today.

Reflecting a tradition of long-standing when something sensational happens, given enough time, stories often slip into the category of folklore. The *West Frankfort Daily American* two days after the Tri-State Tornado related a tale that took place about an hour after the tornado ran south of Dahlgren in Hamilton County. The small agricultural community is sixteen miles southeast of Mt. Vernon, well north of the track. An unnamed farmer was walking his acreage evaluating the damage to his property. He came upon a live, naked baby. "The little one was taken to the farmer's home," the newspaper recounted, "where nourishment and careful attention will preserve

Sightseers at the desks left sitting exactly as they were before the winds hit Braden School. The teacher told students to seek cover under their desks, but some children were strewn around the schoolyard, one suffering injuries serious enough to warrant treatment at the McCoy Library hospital in McLeansboro. *Photo courtesy of the White County (Illinois) Historical Society.*

the life of the [tyke]. It is about three months of age." After an exhaustive search for the parents, it was discovered that the baby rode in the belly of the beast for forty miles. The newspaper said the baby suffered nary a scratch. Neither the name of the farmer nor the name of the baby was disclosed. Was the story factual, or had someone told the reporter a whopper?

A few miles south of Enfield, Illinois, sixteen pupils attended the one-room Trousdale School, built in the middle of horizon-to-horizon corn and soybean fields. One student, Vernon Opal Miller, 12, died from his injuries; his fifteen fellow classmates suffered a ghastly list of wounds, from broken bones to simple cuts and abrasions. Vernon's obituary in the *Carmi Democrat* of March 20 said he enjoyed learning, that he was an eager student, and was now enjoying God's School.

John H. "Strawberry" Wilson, president of the Enfield Township High School Board, was at home with his wife, Mary Jane, and daughters, Rachel and Lucy. Six members of the Wilson family survived, but all would have long recuperations. Despite holding onto doors for dear life, Mary and the girls were carried into the dooryard. While they were gathering their wits, smoke began to spiral from the rubble that had been their home. Missing John and calling out his name repeatedly, they frantically searched what little remained of the house until they spotted his legs sticking out of the cellar hole. All three of the Wilson women pulled with all of their might, but Strawberry Wilson was already dead.[8]

"A child of Mr. and Mrs. Murdach was found over a mile away," the *Carmi Tribune-Times* reported on March 19. "It has been brought to Enfield for treatment." The child must have lived, for no Murdach youngster appeared on the official death roster.

Tornadoes leave unanswerable questions in their path. "The home of Albert Bramlet, considered the most beautiful country home in the county was wrecked," the *Carmi Tribune-Times* said on March 19. "The Bramlets were unhurt and a freak of the storm was that a fresh egg was found lying on the front porch after the tornado." Yet, the same winds in the Seven Mile area embedded a clothespin in a tree and sent a 2 × 4 to pierce a cedar tree to the depth of three inches.

One poor woman was hunkered down in her home, weathering the winds as she had many, many times in a spring storm. A kitchen stove crashed through the roof and crushed her. Mrs. Enos Jordan was crippled for the rest of her life.

The ruins of Lawrence Smith Sr.'s home near the Olga Telephone Exchange in Twigg Township, Hamilton County. Smith survived. Lawrence Jr., who lived nearby, was carried some distance from his house and, although covered in mud, was unhurt. Two rooms of the house were left intact and provided temporary housing to homeless neighbors. *Photo postcard image courtesy of the Hamilton County (Illinois) Historical Society.*

Ruins of the Lick Creek Church in Mayberry Township, Hamilton County. The church was rebuilt by its parishioners. This image gives a sense of the topography typical of this region along the Wabash River drainage. *From a period penny postcard courtesy of the Hamilton County (Illinois) Historical Society.*

Geneva Nipper of the Braden Valley community in Hamilton County was four and disappointed she could not tag along with her older sister, June, to the Braden School. Geneva recalled the sky was green most of the day. The little girl was mollified when her mother consented to making a trip to her grandfather's general store to buy material and a dress pattern for June's fast-approaching last day of school. The hired hand, Roscoe Wooldridge, harnessed a "young span of mules" for the trip. While Geneva and her mother were in the store, the Tri-State hit. "It looked like a big black and green smoke," Geneva said, "rolling on the ground as far as I could see in the valley, rolling trees and every thing in its path." Her mother told how she saw Geneva about three feet off the ground spinning in place like a toy top and finally landing under the feet of the mules. Geneva was rescued by a store customer, Gayle Arms. Her family emerged from the wreckage of their farm and lives with only cuts and bruises.[9]

CROSSVILLE AND WHITE COUNTY, ILLINOIS

White County was a mirror to its neighbor Hamilton County. Agriculture kept both areas going, yet the first twenty-five years of the twentieth century brought a 25 percent decline in population with an estimated density of just fourteen people per square mile. Not many called the small farms that dominated the five-hundred-square-mile bureaucratic entity home. Despite low population density, the sheer width and severity of the tornado was sufficient to destroy 110 farmhouses and 220 outbuildings and kill 38 people and leave 28 listed in serious condition. Enfield Township was the worst with 19 dead. The county lost 3 churches rendered unusable, 8 schools swept away, and a total of $750,000 in damages, the *Carmi Times* reported on March 19.

Witnesses, as reported in the same newspaper, told of cattle and horses taken away on the wind and found muddy but unhurt miles away from their home pastures. Plucked by the winds of every feather on their bodies, those chickens that survived strutted former barnyards naked as the day they were hatched. The Little Wabash River plus countless farm ponds bloated by spring rains were sucked dry as the tornado passed over them. Cancelled checks from the Enfield Bank, a flour sack from a Carmi mill, and a tax receipt from McLeansboro one county over were found in Bicknell, Indiana, a hundred miles northeast. But the most astonishing manifestation was reported by Jaspar Brown of Bumble Bee Bend. He brought to Carmi pieces of wood and tree limbs bristling with straw imbedded by the extreme winds.

Rural one-room schools served the region with one facility every two square miles, an extravagance that yielded to consolidation in the 1950s. With classes in session, Stokes School blew away, then Bell School, then Braden School and the Freiberger School, with more to come. Twenty-one-year-old Scigal Martin, the teacher responsible for the Stokes School, rolled the dice with his students' lives. Sizing up the onrushing storm as abnormally threatening, he ordered everyone to lie in a ditch adjacent to the small building. Not a single student was lost.

Snowden Biggerstaff was not as fortunate. He was the teacher at the Murdach School between Enfield and Carmi. He let his students out for the day upon seeing the dark cloud approaching and was on his way home when the tornado caught up with him. Both his arms were broken as was a leg, which was so traumatized it had to be amputated at the hospital in Evansville, Indiana. He died from his wounds. "His horse had a leg broken," reported the *Carmi Times* the day after the tornado, "and when found the faithful animal was standing over his stricken master." As fate would have it, the Murdach School was not in the path of the tornado.

The Red Cross dispatched eleven nurses to the White County Hospital in Carmi and placed field nurse McGreavy in charge. The *Carmi Times-Tribune* reported on March 19, "There is no charge whatever at the hospital and injured are urged to come there for care. . . . Only one death has occurred at the hospital since the storm and that death was expected as the patient had a fractured skull." The Red Cross shipped by train to Carmi relief supplies amounting to 1,350 blankets, a hundred tents, four hundred cots, a hundred cook stoves, ten outdoor cooking kits, and household furnishings. As with other railroad lines in the region, the Louisville and Nashville Railroad carted the materials pro bono.[10] By Friday, Sears-Roebuck of Chicago delivered freight cars filled with new clothing.

A biplane piloted by Frank O'Neil out of Vincennes, Indiana, on its way to relief headquarters in Carbondale, touched down in Carmi. The biplane carried Sam Guard of the Sears-Roebuck Foundation and E. G. Thiem of the *Prairie Farmer*, a widely read agriculture periodical. Thiem accomplished one of his missions, to fly over every mile of the storm track in Illinois and Indiana, but his most important goal was to set up an office, which he did in Benton, for the Illinois Committee for Rural Relief intended to augment local efforts by the Red Cross and the Salvation Army. Donning the obligatory helmet and goggles for air safety in the open cockpits of the day, Thiem then surveyed the tornado's path between Gorham and Murphysboro; the biplane touched down in an open clover field, fueling up after someone made a run to the nearest gas station. He viewed the heartbreak that was DeSoto and the mile after mile of farms turned into a Titan's game of jackstraws. Thiem commented that the city of Carbondale was alive with activity: people searching for relatives, Red Cross officials scurrying off in every direction, and armed soldiers guarding railroad sheds filled with relief supplies. The center of operations seemed to be the Methodist Church on Main Street. He concluded an extensive story on his experiences: "The plum trees and daffodils are blooming in southern Illinois. They are in season to cover the graves of the hundreds of dead."[11]

The last Illinois town to confront the wind was Crossville, four miles from Indiana. To the south the tornado raged close by the small farming community. Howard Rawlinson sat on the third floor of Crossville Community High School and watched the storm. Although he did not know it at the time, in harm's way were two cousins working in an underground potato cellar, cutting eyes from budded potatoes in preparation for spring planting. The ruckus overhead too much to ignore, one of the young men, consumed by curiosity, opened the cellar door only to be immediately decapitated. He was Fred Bennett, twenty-two.[12]

Rawlinson recounted how he and his classmates organized into groups to search for victims and survivors. In the midst of the debris field, they found a barbed-wire fence rolled into a ball whose interior contained a featherless chicken very much alive. A relative of Howard, Edna Ethel Rawlinson, told a reporter working for the *Carmi Times* that her house was just out of the reach of the worst winds. Her home sustained little damage, but hail the size of teacups peppered the dooryard followed by a "blood red" setting sun that stained the western horizon.[13]

Maimed animals despoiled muddy fields soon to be planted in corn; one was a Jersey milk cow whose belly was pierced by a 2 × 4. But the most horrific sight was an impaled woman's body pinned high in the crotch of a monumental sycamore tree, reported Arthur H. Schneff of the *St. Louis Post-Dispatch* on March 20.

In Phillips Township, Schneff wrote, Ben Kallenbach's place, close to the Skillet Fork River right where it merged with the Little Wabash, became yet another debris field. His friend John Winter, with whom he had gone to an auction sale that day, was dead. Jasper Brown's place on the Bumble Bee Bend of the meandering Little Wabash River was next, then Harvey Graves's, and Bill Moser's, Joe Ridenour's farm, and the Stokes homestead, where James Stokes's wife, Elma, died of her injuries. A collie came crashing through the front window of Pink and Effie Young's farmhouse and survived.[14]

Harry and Barbara Maurer tenant farmed for James Garner, close to the Wabash River. Their house was turned into matchsticks that quickly caught fire. Harry was blown clear of the farmhouse and barn. In shock, he ran back to the clutter that used to be where his family lived. Smoke was everywhere. He heard cries for help from his son, Herschel, coming from the debris-filled cellar hole. One of Herschel's hands was burned, but, otherwise, he was fine, but his mother was nowhere to be found. They did not locate her until the next day. After the fire burned out, Barb Maurer's partially cremated body was uncovered in the cellar hole.[15]

Over the bluffs that demark productive bottomlands on the western side of the Wabash River, the storm continued to be glued to the ground and crossed Pure Road, where another ten farms and Poplar Ridge School were erased. After almost three hours, the killing of unwitting southern Illinoisans persisted when Fairzine Fitzgerald died in the arms of her husband, Kelly, amidst the wreckage of their lives.[16] She was the final fatality in Illinois.

As though a biblical conflagration was on the march toward them that cold and tragic night, a glow of unknown origin in the northeast sky deeply disturbed White County survivors. It was much like that reported in Zeigler, where the pulsing glow was caused by the fires devouring Murphysboro and DeSoto. White County had no way of knowing it, but a mere five miles away a sister Indiana town was ablaze.

GRIFFIN, INDIANA

As soon as the storm reached the Wabash River around 4 P.M., the Tri-State Tornado changed for the first time since its beginning in the Missouri Ozarks. Still a mile-wide F5, the forward speed inexplicably accelerated to match the seventy-three miles per hour last registered as it crossed the Mississippi River, a speed faster than the most sophisticated contemporary steam locomotive in the world.

Drenched by heavy rains for weeks before the storm arrived, the Wabash River was over its banks as were numerous small tributaries that laced the area, adding even greater problems to the disaster. This extreme-southwest corner of Indiana with its notably fertile farmland was known as the Pocket. As soon as the tornado ran over the black Indiana soil, another change occurred. No longer was the vortex filled with just dirt. It was now stuffed with lowland mud plus all the water pulled into the vortex from rivers, creeks, and farm ponds. Less than four minutes after crossing the Wabash River, the tornado was on the outskirts of a crossroads town first platted in 1875, Griffin, Indiana, whose four hundred souls had nary an inkling of the devastation to come.

Seventeen-year-old Orval Carter watched the tornado from the relative safety of a vantage point in open country a half mile from the track. He ran to Griffin to do what he could and found the town completely destroyed.

Devastation at Griffin, Indiana, from a perspective outside the town. The photo was probably snapped by someone touring the storm track. *Original photo courtesy of the Hamilton County (Illinois) Historical Society.*

"Everything was strewn around; bodies, trees, and houses," he told a *St. Louis Post-Dispatch* reporter. A fire in the middle of town was consuming Griffin's only restaurant, Kokomoor's, owned by Dr. and Mrs. Kokomoor. Like so many other horrific stories from Gorham's Wallace's Restaurant to the Blue Front Hotel in Murphysboro, would-be rescuers were stymied. "From the remains of the building we heard screams," said Carter, one of the would-be rescuers. "We tried to reach them but the flames drove us back."

Nine people were inside, two Kokomoors—Flo and her daughter, Mary—and seven customers, one of whom was nineteen-year-old Thomas Nottingham, whose father worked desperately to free his son. All nine died in hellish agony, their partially cremated bodies found huddled together behind a potbelly stove.[17] Two of the boys were burned so badly relatives were forced to use the marbles and penknives in pants' pockets to identify the owners.

Clarence Combs was another Griffin resident trapped in a burning building. A heavy rock pinned his foot. He, too, was burned alive. Seven people entombed in the collapsed post office perished similarly. The reek of burning flesh would never be forgotten by those who lived to tell their stories.

School had dismissed at its usual time of 3:45 P.M. The horse-drawn bus used to cart the children was well on its appointed rounds with the second and final load of six children. Out in the open, the wind buffeting the vehicle, the driver could not hold the bus on the road. The horse was skittish, the children terrified, but the only adult in the bus showed courage when he went to the back exit, opened the door, and stepped down. That was the last the children saw of him. He was picked up by the wind as were the children. The driver, the horse, and two of the six youngsters died.[18]

Unrelenting rains that followed the mayhem helped to eventually quench the fires but not before 25 people died and 202 were injured, giving Griffin the dubious distinction of experiencing the highest casualty rate of any town overrun by the tornado—57 percent. "Those injured by the storm were so dazed they could not even remember where their homes had been," reported the *Kokomo (IN) Daily Tribune* on March 20. "They wandered about aimlessly unable to leave . . . unable to help themselves." Many could not recall the names of their children or spouse. They were covered with slimy, black mud rained on Griffin by the storm, one witness saying Griffin could have been mistaken as a "negro town."

"At daylight Red Cross workers, Evansville firemen and policemen, state troopers and others resumed the gruesome task of hunting the dead," the Kokomo paper said. Indiana National Guardsmen of Battery E of the 139th Field Artillery stationed in Indianapolis roadblocked all entrances to Griffin to prevent looting as well as to control the inevitable onslaught of sightseers. Like Gorham and Parrish, the first relief arrived by train. The National Guard brought tents for temporary shelter in which some families without financial reserves lived for more than a year. "Scores of nurses and physicians co-operating with Miss Grace Wright, federal Red Cross agent here, have been rushed [to the scene] in taxicabs, ambulances, and special trains," the *Logansport (IN) Morning Press* related on March 19. The brand-new Ribeye Gym in New Harmony performed its first civic service by acting as Griffin's hospital and morgue. None of the original eighty structures in Griffin survived intact. Most were unsalvageable or simply no longer existed.

Rains continued, so much so Griffin quickly developed another emergency. By Friday, the turbid waters of the Wabash threatened to isolate what was left. While visiting Griffin that day, Indiana governor Edward Jackson, an avowed member of the Ku Klux Klan, was nearly trapped by the waters. By nightfall, the only way in or out was by skiff or railroad. Red Cross relief supplies that were to be delivered by truck were delayed and had to reach Griffin by railcar.

Griffin was eventually put back together and is a viable small town today with about half the population it had in 1925. Basketball is like an organized religion in Indiana. Unbroken townspeople decided to change the name of their teams. The junior high and grade schools became the Whirlwinds and the high school the Tornadoes.

Beyond Griffin, the tornado changed again, the Logansport paper continued, "turning slightly northward which set it on a dead-ahead course for the [Indiana] towns of Owensville and Princeton," the latter being the populous seat of government for Gibson County and the third-largest town in the storm track. "No longer a mile wide . . . the cloud appeared to be trying to [compensate] for its diminishing [width] by increasing its forward speed," observed author Peter Felknor in his 1992 book *The Tri-State Tornado*.[19]

OWENSVILLE, INDIANA

At 4:11 P.M., the tornado reached the southwest periphery of Owensville, the worst of the winds depredating farmlands south of town. The death count in Owensville reached seventeen. Eyewitness reports differ as to the shape of the storm at this stage in its long and dreadful life. Some said it was now three contiguous funnels; others described a wall cloud providing a black veil for an enormous single vortex.[20]

During the search for survivors, a baby was found in a creek. No one claimed the infant. The King family of Owensville lost four family members to the wind.

The Waters family had for years owned a farm outside Owensville. Three generations of Waters died that Wednesday when their farmhouse disintegrated; the patriarch of the family, Richard, seventy, his six-year-old grandson, two grown sons—one named Lemuel, who was father to the dead child—and their wives died of injuries.[21]

As with other towns that day, public buildings became temporary hospitals and morgues. Such was the case with the Crossville Public Library. Once patients were stabilized, they were transported to Evansville, twenty-eight miles south.

From Griffin to Owensville to the outskirts of Princeton, another eighty-five farms were annihilated.

PRINCETON, INDIANA

Ten minutes after Crossville, at 4:22 P.M., without warning, the Tri-State entered the southwest quadrant of Princeton. Residents in the north part of town, like those in the south of West Frankfort, had no inkling what had hit the city of sixty-five hundred. Telephones began to ring throughout Princeton, and emergency sirens could be heard wailing and heading south along Main, Seminary, and Hart Streets. Battered cars filled with dead or injured sought hospitals and doctor's offices.

Like Murphysboro, Princeton was a railroad town, serviced agricultural businesses in the region, offered steady coal mining work, and was the most important financial center between Terre Haute to the north and Evansville on the Ohio River to the south. Princeton was more fortunate than Gorham, Murphysboro, and DeSoto. Luckily, schoolchildren had time to get home. The Baldwin Heights School lost its roof and most of the second floor. Many of the nearly five hundred students would have lost their lives in the brick school had the tornado gotten there at the end of the school day, as was the case in DeSoto.

One of Princeton's largest employers was the H. J. Heinz Corporation's ketchup plant. Most of the workers lived in proximity to their jobs. Survivors told of thinking the black clouds were the usual spring thunderstorms. After all, Wednesday had been prematurely warm. Ventilation windows were opened in the Heinz greenhouses to prevent the growing space for tomato plants from overheating.

Whole worlds flew apart in less than a minute, leaving lives changed forever. Forty-five Princeton citizens died, and 152 were injured, the worst Tri-State death total for any Indiana town. The most concentrated losses were to the neat rows of small bungalows housing Heinz employees near the factory.

"I was getting ready to go get my check that day," said Blanche Giesel-man, "and the office was a small building out away from the main plant, and of course [the tornado] blew the office away. They had the checks in there on the cabinet. All our checks blew away, but they was in a bundle and had an elastic band around them, and they found them up around West Baden [fifty-five miles northeast of Princeton]. We got back the original checks!" One fatality occurred within the plant. Gieselman said the woman "started to the front end and a piece of timber hit her in the throat and killed her right there."[22]

The 4 P.M. shift had just begun. "We had seventy-five persons, men and women in the factory," said E. F. Felts, superintendent, "and about fifteen in the greenhouse. The force of the wind . . . drove the employees into the [lower level of the] new building where they were in comparative safety." Many employees escaped injury in a warehouse area stacked with large, square tin cans filled with tomato concentrate. The cans supported metal girders under the collapsed roof and prevented the girders from falling on frightened men and women.[23]

Twenty-year-old new mother Olive Deffendall of Princeton recalled lis-tening to the workers through windows flung open for sweet spring-fresh air. Unbeknownst to those in its path, the storm approached at breakneck speed. The men were walking up Seminary Street from the rail yard and factories; some were swinging their dinner buckets over their heads and enjoying their freedom as much as the early spring weather. They were "singing and prancing," in high spirits. That was until Olive turned and saw the cloud. "Of course, I didn't know what it was," she said. "It was black and red and orange and purple, rolling over and over like a barrel. The underneath was a dusky yellow." She called to her friend Ella Beasely in the kitchen, making biscuits for supper to come see the beautiful cloud. Just then, "[a] two-burner stove came in through the dining room window and sat right down in the middle of the table."[24]

Mildred Field was a nineteen-year-old Heinz employee. As they often did, she and a coworker friend walked the mile home together when the weather was nice. Caught in the open, Mildred wrapped her arms around a street-lamp pole and yelled above the roar for her younger friend to grab onto her waist. Holding on for dear life, the two were lifted parallel to the ground. Her friend slipped off. Mildred came through wet and scared but untouched. Despite weeks in the hospital, her friend spent the rest of her life in a wheelchair.[25]

The Heinz facility lost its warehouse, engine room, business offices, and greenhouse and was reduced from two stories to one. Management was quick to inform Princeton the factory would be rebuilt. H. J. Heinz was true to their word.

The Southern Railway repair facility was left in ruin, too. Gone were the machine and blacksmith shops, the roundhouse, and office buildings. Most men had already left for home so the Dante-esque scenes experienced in the M&O yards at Murphysboro were not repeated. Also not repeated was the corporate duplicity Murphysboro experienced when M&O brass pledged to rebuild the yards only to retract the statement during the Christmas season. Only two lives were lost at the Princeton yard, a janitor and a fireman. None of the four hundred to five hundred jobs were lost. Estimates ran as high as $1 million to rehabilitate the facility that Southern Railway rebuilt.

Red Cross and National Guard aid quickly arrived in Princeton. Local relief workers in the city were praised by Red Cross director Henry Baker for their efficiency and quick response.

Soon enough, the tornado continued northeast of Princeton for another fifteen miles. Once beyond the city limits, it shrunk by 50 percent to a half-mile across, but wind velocity ramped. Even though the tornado was nearing dissipation, another dozen farms were demolished.[26]

At approximately 4:30 P.M. in open farmland near Petersburg, Indiana, after traveling on the ground for three and a half hours covering 219 miles, the Tri-State Tornado was rapidly losing power. In a curious bit of ironic symmetry, its onset was witnessed by a postman outside Ellington, Missouri; its ending was observed and reported by rural Indiana mail carrier E. E. Williams. After spinning itself into history as the deadliest tornado ever in the United States and the third worst in the recorded story of all mankind, the Tri-State Tornado roped out and disappeared.

6

▼

Aftermath

I t has been said that the measure of a person may be drawn by how well he or she performs in adversity. People in the three-state region, particularly Egypt because it experienced 80 percent of the total casualties, had an enormous problem on their hands. Medical care, drugs, hospital beds, and supplies of all kinds must be brought in. Immediate shelter needed to be created and quickly for the thousands dispossessed by the tornado. Plans had to be made to rebuild permanent homes. With an estimated $12 million in damage in southern Illinois alone, 695 dead, 15,000 buildings no longer useable, and more than 10,000 people homeless, the task must have seemed impossible. Rutted roads were clogged with traffic; electric, telegraph, and telephone lines were down. The Red Cross and the National Guard coordinated shipping from Chicago canvas military tents for lodging, warming stoves, four thousand pillows, clothing, food, hospital supplies, blood, four thousand bed sacks, wound-dressing stations, potable drinking water; all were provided free of charge. At its peak, the relief effort delivered daily aid to twenty-five thousand.[1]

The green shoots of economic and cultural growth often sprout from tragedy, but the reverse often happens, too. So it was for those affected by the Tri-State Tornado in Egypt. With the help of burgeoning technologies, the region rolled up its figurative sleeves and went to work. Such modern instruments as the telephone, the radio, and the airplane all played starring roles in the recovery as did organizations, such as the Red Cross, the military, and corporate America, but none would be enough to lift Egypt permanently. Like Rocky Balboa's strategy to wear down Apollo Creed with body blows, the Tri-State Tornado softened southern Illinois, drained scarce capital, and set it up for a fall. The destruction of whole villages and towns that were never rejuvenated and in the case of Parrish, Illinois, never rebuilt began a slow regional denouement. Whole sections of Egypt became increasingly poor and isolated. Had infrastructure stayed intact, perhaps history would have been different, and the region would be more prosperous than it is. In the course of rebuilding, life savings were depleted or exhausted. Unlike today when the federal government offers low-interest loans to disaster survivors, local banks were the only source of borrowed capital in a time when loans were hard to come by and not a common part of family or business balance sheets.

Unemployed coal miner and his dog, in Bush, Illinois, January 1939. An iconic image and one of the best-known of Arthur Rothstein's photographs, this staged scene captures the dejection of being without a job. The only one who seems to care about the man is his mutt. *From Herbert Russell,* A Southern Illinois Album: Farm Security Administration Photographs, 1936–1943 *(Carbondale: Southern Illinois University Press, 1990), 40.*

In four years, the Great Depression's grip on the United States accelerated Egypt's decline. Coal mines closed, railroads declared bankruptcy, or, as was the case with the M&O in Murphysboro even before the Great Depression, companies acted dishonorably by permanently eliminating jobs. Many undercapitalized small banks in Egypt shuttered their doors, leaving depositors with no recourse to recover savings. The money simply did not exist anymore.

The widow Minnie Barnett, raising a family of four in DeSoto, is a perfect example of living conditions in southern Illinois soon after the Tri-State Tornado wiped the village off the face of the earth. That they survived is inspiring. That they did not prosper is both indicative and tragic. "We got by" is what Betty Barnett Moroni told the author about how her family made it through such difficult times. Minimizing the effort, yet with familial pride shining in her eyes, she said, "We got by, is all."

METEOROLOGICAL EXPLANATION OF THE TRI-STATE TORNADO

Murphysboro-born professor Wallace Akin made the observation that the supercell which developed into the third worst in world history was an astonishing formation triple the size normally capable of producing a tornado. The average tornado's track on the ground is about 6 miles. The Tri-State's was 219 miles with an average width as much as twelve times normal. Akin explains,

> [A] more concrete bit of data comes from the office of Old Ben Mine no. 8. There an operating barograph—an instrument for measuring and recording atmospheric pressure—logged the passage of the Tornado only one mile north of the mine. It produced a piece of paper . . . that . . . confirms that at West Frankfort the center of this great cyclonic system and the tornado arrived together. . . . [T]he presence of the Tornado near the center of the cyclonic system . . . contributed to its great power and long life. Most supercells and accompanying tornadoes develop much farther south . . . in the warm air ahead of the cold front.

The barometric reading, taken a mile away, sank sharply as the vortex passed, bottoming at an astounding 28.7 inches of mercury.[2]

Frustration over the inability to warn those who might lie in the terrible storm's path as well as to communicate the seriousness of the terrible storm to those who might help must have been high. Downed telegraph and telephone lines cannot carry signals. Few of the counties in the tornado's track had organized civil defense systems ready to spring into action. As imaging technology improved, particularly radar after World War II, forecasting techniques became more and more sophisticated. The shocking number of deaths from the Tri-State pushed the National Weather Bureau to begin a program to train storm spotters, which is still an integral part of today's warning systems. Interestingly, a tornado's signature "hook" pattern was tracked for the first time on radar in 1953 by staff at the Illinois State Water Survey in Springfield. The feat led to national development of early-warning radar sites much like those used by NORAD (North American Aerospace Command) during the Cold War to detect Soviet missile launches headed for the United States over the North Pole. Since 1925, vast improvements have been made to increase the safety of those in harm's way.

Today, of course, the supercell would have been spotted, labeled, and warned of by every media outlet in the area, but such was not the case in 1925, an era when phones were still a technological rarity in Egypt. Page 53 shows the DeSoto schoolhouse prior to the storm; no phone line or electric power line enters the building.

Nationalized standard guidelines for the physical safety of students during a tornado were discussed at local, state, and federal levels, and a wholly new set of safety protocols established. Indeed, the randomness and off-the cuff nature of each school's preparedness reaction to the Tri-State are shocking. In addition, civil engineers were sent to Egypt to analyze the variable damage patterns to the spectrum of building designs found in the region. This survey would lay the groundwork for better and more durable public building construction techniques that focus on the use of steel backbones within brick structures to prevent the catastrophic collapse of brick buildings as seen in Murphysboro and DeSoto.

AIRPLANES

World War I inaugurated the historic use of airplanes in combat as well as use for rapid transportation of important materials and as surveillance platforms, dirigible destruction, messaging, artillery spotters, intelligence collection, use as air ambulances, and transport of critical personnel. For the first time in American history, in the wake of the Tri-State Tornado, flight played a crucial role in a natural disaster recovery effort.

The night of the storm, William Fortune, Indiana Red Cross director, received an emergency telegram from Red Cross Disaster Relief headquarters in Carbondale requesting any and all supplies of tetanus antitoxin be sent as quickly as possible. Thousands of lives were at risk. The ravaged region had exhausted all local supplies as well as those in St. Louis. Fortune phoned Brigadier General Dwight Aultman, the commandant of Fort Benjamin Harrison, a US Army base outside of Indianapolis, Indiana, with a growing army air wing. They decided to contact Eli Lilly and Company, whose world headquarters and one of its pharmaceutical plants were in Indianapolis. The plant manager was asked to begin immediate production of the serum. Realizing the seriousness of the request, Lilly shut down all other operations to concentrate on the task. By sunrise Friday, 750 "tubes" of serum were produced. The vaccine left the army airbase with army officers R. H. Stewart, a local man from Indianapolis, and Harry Miles, of Dayton, Ohio, at the controls of a biplane headed to relief headquarters in Carbondale. They landed on a strip of pasture north of town along the Illinois Central tracks where Carbondale's industrial park is located today.[3]

St. Louis also played a role in the airlift of emergency supplies when a biplane took off from Bridgeton Field (later to become Lambert Field–St. Louis) with 225,000 units of tetanus antitoxin made by the Parke-Davis Company, America's largest pharmaceutical company of the day. Parke-Davis officials were on hand when the plane touched down in Mt. Vernon.[4]

On March 13, 1925, just five days before the Tri-State spawned, Charles Lindbergh, the great American aviation pioneer, earned his wings at Kelly Field, a US Air Service Flying School, in San Antonio, Texas. The army did not need active pilots so the new second lieutenant joined the 110th Observation Squadron, 35th Division of the Missouri Air National Guard unit back home in St. Louis and was made a first lieutenant. Lindbergh did what other unemployed pilots in love with the airplane did at the time. He barnstormed and worked as a flight instructor, picking up whatever jobs he could find.

Chicagoan Henry Schaefer, a representative of the Pacific and Atlantic Photos Corporation, a division of the *Chicago Tribune* and its sister paper, the *Daily News* of New York City, arrived at work in the Chicago Tribune Tower on March 19, 1925, at his accustomed 8:00 A.M. He was surprised to see his boss, bureau chief Henry Allison, on the phone to the newspaper's St. Louis operations, urgently looking for a pilot for a sensitive and important assignment. The *Tribune* sent a photographer to Egypt on the Illinois Central on the night of the eighteenth with instructions to snap as many pictures as possible as soon as the sun rose.

Allison finally made arrangements with none other than the dependable Charles Lindbergh, who rented a plane to fly to Murphysboro to pick up the state-of-the-art camera's 4-inch × 5-inch glass plates from the *Tribune* photographer. Lindbergh was instructed to meet the photographer at the

Charles Lindbergh adjusting a parachute at Bridgton Field—now Lambert International Airport—before flight testing an experimental biplane in St. Louis, 1925. Lindbergh would have flown this type of open-cockpit aircraft from St. Louis to Murphysboro the day after the Tri-State Tornado. *Postcard in the author's collection.*

Western Union office on Walnut Street. When Lindbergh arrived at the office, a man sitting by the window with a package in his lap rose when Lindbergh asked the clerk to point out the *Tribune* man. The package was handed over, and the man instructed Lindbergh to fly as fast as he could to Chicago to deliver the plates.

He arrived at Checkerboard Field in Maywood, a field Lindbergh would use regularly beginning April 1926 when he was hired by the US Postal Service to fly regular airmail runs from St. Louis to Chicago. So valuable were the photo plates that the *Tribune* sent three bodyguards to accompany him downtown. The plates were immediately surrendered to the *Tribune*'s most seasoned film developer.

Speed was what Henry Allison hoped to gain by hiring Lindbergh, speed with which the editor could smoke his fiercest competitor, William Randolph Hearst, and his *Herald Examiner* and afternoon edition, the *New York Journal American*.

His face ashen, the staff developer returned to Allison's office to tell him not a single picture appeared on any of the photographic plates. Lindbergh and the *Tribune* had been duped. It was learned later that a Hearst organization man had discovered the *Tribune*'s plan and given Lindbergh the unexposed plates.

Lindbergh was notoriously cool to the press throughout his very public life, ironic since he was this country's first mass-media star. One has to wonder if his antipathy, his open distrust's wellspring were tapped in the Western Union office on Walnut Street in the midst of the smoldering wreckage of Murphysboro.[5]

Not to be outdone by aggressive midwestern papers, *New York Times* editors, when news came in that an independent St. Louis cameraman had made a trip to Murphysboro to film the devastation, placed a *Times* cameraman onboard a biplane with pilot Joe James and a reporter taking notes on a typewriter on his lap. The day after the Tri-State ripped through Murphysboro, James took off from Checkerboard Field. At a cruising speed of ninety miles an hour, the flight would have taken more than three cold hours to reach Murphysboro. James circled the flattened city while the cameraman shot 16 mm, soundless movies. They then wheeled northeast to wing over DeSoto. The appalling images played as a devilish prelude to silent movies all over the world.[6]

RADIO, TELEPHONE, AND FILM TECHNOLOGY

With the advent in 1922 of clear-channel radio stations of immense power able to carry signals great distances, news could travel at the speed of light, and because of it, the Tri-State Tornado was the first national tragedy with near-instantaneous reporting. More and more, people were turning to the radio for breaking news stories, entertainment, and the latest information from around the world. The *New York Times* devoted nearly a full page each edition to give readers programming schedules from stations across the country.

A survivor recuperating in the temporary hospital in the Murphysboro Eagles Lodge received a cablegram from relatives in Germany inquiring about his status. They said they learned of the disaster on German radio.

Radio offered continuous reporting on the freshest developments in the tornado's story. Newspapers were limited to one or, at best, two editions a day. With the advent of the mass production of the amplifying vacuum tube by such companies as Westinghouse, AT&T, and Radio Corporation of America, a wireless world began to dawn in earnest in 1925. Reflecting that development, in February the *Carbondale Free Press* ran a story that listed thirty-six radio stations available from across the nation, their call letters, and dial settings. KMOX in St. Louis was the closest to Egypt.

Radio is credited with the dissemination of early news of the disaster that helped to quickly bring military and medical personnel from as far away as Chicago, three hundred miles to the north. In addition, European radio stations carried the news of the great destruction, causing relatives of area residents to cable the American Red Cross in an avalanche of requests urgently seeking the status of their relations.

A March 20 special dispatch to the *St. Louis Globe-Democrat* reported, "[E]very radio station in Chicago abandoned regular programs Wednesday night and today to give what aid it could and all day thousands of dollars poured into different radio studios as a result of the appeals for funds." The same edition reported that the *Chicago Tribune* opened a two-way radio connection with southern Illinois.

In the Egypt of 1925, radio in this rural area was hardly widespread. In 1939, WEBQ in Harrisburg, Illinois, became the first AM station in southern Illinois.[7]

Isaac K. Levy, Murphysboro's relief committee chairman, received a handwritten letter from "a long-lost relation" in Chicago in which Dan D. Lichtenstein offered Levy and his family an empty bungalow he owned in Maywood, Illinois, near Chicago. "I have sent word to you," Levy's cousin said, "and the rest of the folks by radio from station WLS but have received no reply."[8] With gratitude in his written message back to his cousin, Levy declined the offer.

Technology was also changing news imaging. Newspaper readers clamored for photographs of the breathtaking destruction. In 1924, the St. Louis *Post-Dispatch* introduced a brand-new wireless information transmission system capable of sending images electronically over long distances. The technology, owned exclusively by the St. Louis paper and Joseph Pulitzer's *New York World*, furnished dramatic images instantly for an international and news-hungry public. The transmission of the heartbreaking photos, a delivery that would have taken more than twenty-four hours by train to New York, now required little more than ten minutes' preparation time to cross the thousand miles.

Betty Moroni's family of eight did not own a phone or a radio at the time of the storm. DeSoto did, however, have a telephone exchange where operators manipulated line and plug walls connecting callers to ubiquitous party lines. The two-story switching building, sheathed in buff tiles common in southern Illinois construction, was referred to as the "Yellow Building." It was demolished by the Tri-State. Betty Moroni and her husband, Jesse, bought the vacant lot where the exchange once stood and built a home on it in the 1950s. She still lives in the home.

Fresh from medical school in 1921, Dr. C. H. Williams moved to West Frankfort to begin the practice of medicine. "There were very few telephones out there in those days," he said in a July 7, 1978, interview. His story is indicative of the dearth of modern technology available in the Egypt of the 1920s. "The [Orient mines] operators couldn't call me if I was making house calls so they devised a plan to let me know if I was needed. The mine [steam] whistle blew four blasts if a doctor was needed." A more elaborate system had been in place for years. Three blasts at 4 P.M. indicated the mine would work the next day. No one wanted the whistle to shrill once for that meant the mine was closed the next day but even more dreaded were continuous short blasts to warn that an accident had occurred and fathers were surely dead.[9] In many ways this was still the railroad era, although as we will see in Murphysboro, trains were losing their transportation preeminence to cars, truck, and busses. Most railroads prided themselves on staying on schedule no matter what the weather or time of day. People in small-town America listened for the noon train whistle as it crossed Main Street, or the garment factory steam whistle announcing shift changes at regular hours, or church bells tolling the hour and if it was a prosperous parish the half and quarter, too.

"Moving pictures" enjoyed a thriving business in southern Illinois. Egyptians were just as interested as anyone in the country in the happenings of Tinseltown and to see such silent screen stars as the zany Harold Lloyd, that lovable Tramp Charlie Chaplin, and the bewitching Clara Bow. Benton, Illinois, a city of eight thousand north of West Frankfort, supported two theaters, the Star and the Capitol. In the March 24 *Benton Evening News*, an announcement appeared that the manager of the theaters, "Keibley, a live wire, ever alert to the best and latest motion pictures, true to form, has secured for the first presentation in Illinois authentic pictures of the storm-stricken towns in Southern Illinois and they will be shown at the Capitol and Star Theatres tonight only."

GOVERNMENT INVOLVEMENT AND CHARITABLE GIVING

In the early decades of the twentieth century, the country was without any official social safety net administered by the US government. Families and individuals alike were largely on their own. Relief agencies like the Red Cross gave significant help to those affected by the storm as did the National Guard. Volunteer medical personnel from all over Egypt as well as the cities of Chicago and St. Louis came to help.

Championed by Governor Len Small, the Illinois legislature created a $500,000 fund to assist victims. The City of Chicago pledged another $500,000 and ended up giving close to $1 million. Boy Scouts and Girl Scouts all across the country as well as churches, fraternal orders, clubs, sororities, and labor unions solicited donations. WLS radio, Chicago's dominant station, collected $112,299 from its listeners. The Red Cross accepted millions of dollars from public donations, but the help was meant to be temporal to uplift the lives of damaged men, women, and children who were actively attempting to make their lives whole again. Once that mission was completed, relief efforts were over.

In a small but heartfelt gesture typical of the era, the on-tour New York City Police Band, on their way to Chicago, stopped at Murphysboro on the Friday after the storm. The bandleader handed Mayor Gus Blair $150 collected from their receipts in Memphis, Tennessee, the night before. They pledged to Blair 100 percent of the gate for an upcoming Chicago concert.

The St. Louis Fruit and Produce Association shipped five railroad cars packed with fruits and vegetables. Belleville schoolchildren collected fifteen truckloads of used clothing, shoes, and hats that the Air Corps at Scott Field trucked to Carbondale. A Nashua, New Hampshire, woolen mill shipped more than eight tons of blankets to Egypt.

Five days after the storm, Ike Levy entreated the nation via the Associated Press, Reuters, and United Press. Powerful in its passion, the message in its entirety was printed on the front page of the *Daily Independent* on March 26.

AN APPEAL TO THE NATION

The nation at large cannot fully realize or appreciate the great loss and damage that the people of Murphysboro and vicinity have sustained as a result of the terrible storm of last Wednesday, and of the fire which followed. The consequences are staggering. The loss of life is great and the number of people suffering from personal injuries is enormous. The loss of property is . . . so complete that a personal visit to the stricken area is necessary to comprehend our present predicament.

The actual needs of our people are so great that the burden should not be borne by a few communities but by the whole nation. I believe it is fitting and proper that local relief committees be formed and that a representative be sent from each of such organizations for the purpose of making a personal investigation and inspection of our situation, and after the report is made to take such action in the premises as they feel circumstances warrant.

We want to pay whatever funds and money you subscribe and raise to responsible organizations and to responsible persons who will see to it that the money is judiciously spent and our homeless and stricken people are given the full benefit of every dollar.

It is not charity that we are seeking. Our actual wants, needs, and necessities compel us to make this appeal.

Signed Isaac K. Levy, General Chairman Relief Committee

Levy also quickly went to work finding the funds with which to re-build their schools. Logan and Longfellow were obviously never going to be used again, and the high school needed extensive refurbishment before it was habitable.

To his dismay, Levy discovered that the Red Cross's charter forbade school reconstruction. Adding further roadblocks, the schools in Murphys-boro were bonded to the statutory limit after the aggressive expansion of the high school only a year before the storm. Much of the personal and real property upon which the city taxed residents for operating revenue, debt amortization, and retirement had been destroyed.[10]

Inexplicably, at first, the state superintendent of schools Francis G. Blair blocked all legislative appropriations. Instead, he devised a plan to tax teachers and students throughout the state to pay for their brothers' and sisters' recuperation. Teachers were to pay $1, high school pupils fifty cents, grade schoolers a dime, and the state universities $10,000. Blair figured this self-reliant system would raise $255,000. A frustrated Levy turned to state senators Richard Meents of Ashkum and Harry Watson to sponsor an appropriation bill for $275,000. In time, under intense public pressure, Superintendent Blair backed off. The bill passed in May. Murphysboro could begin rebuilding its schools.[11]

Levy wrote impassioned pleas for cash with which to rebuild the schools of his city. The Illinois appropriation pushed through the legislature by the governor, generous as it was, made no provision for that purpose. Letters asking for help went to Henry Ford, Russell Sage, Julius Rosenwald, part-owner of Sears, Roebuck, and Company in Chicago, Andrew Carnegie, and John D. Rockefeller of Standard Oil. Only Rockefeller, who knew southern Illinois well, responded positively with a $5,000 check from Standard Oil. Rockefeller had personally scouted the area preliminary to opening the Illi-nois Basin to oil exploration, where oil wells can be seen pumping yet today.

THE RED CROSS

Known as the "angel of the battlefield" for her tireless work with wounded Civil War soldiers, former schoolteacher Clara Barton founded the American Red Cross in 1881. The following year, the Geneva Convention was ratified. The Red Cross received a congressional charter in 1900 to uphold the tenets of the Geneva Convention as well as provide aid to American armed forces and their families. The organization was also chartered to provide national and international natural disaster relief. All services were to be funded entirely by private donations.

Prior to the Tri-State, the Red Cross succored hurricane victims in Galveston, Texas, in 1900, a natural horror show where estimates range between 6,000 and 10,000 Americans died. The Red Cross was on scene following the San Francisco Earthquake of 1906, where the estimated death toll was 3,000, and would return to Egypt and the south to assist victims of the Great Mississippi River Flood of 1927 when the Red Cross provided services for 637,000 people and inoculated 457,000. The flood displaced an estimated 700,000 Americans. Only insofar as the National Guard was called to duty by the representative governors of each effected state, the US government played only a minimal role in recovery efforts.

Thursday morning, March 19, President Calvin Coolidge learned his father, John, had just suffered two heart attacks back in Plymouth Notch, Vermont. In the same White House briefing, the president was informed of the Tri-State Tornado. Small-government advocate and business friendly Coolidge acted as both president of the United States and the honorary chairman of the board of the Red Cross when he penned this characteristically succinct note to the Red Cross president.

The White House
Washington, DC

My Dear Judge Payne
Information has reached me of a disaster that has overtaken a portion of Missouri, Illinois, and Indiana. It is said that many people are homeless and many are injured. I suggest that you put in operation all the facilities of the Red Cross to assist in the required relief. I am sending a telegram to the Governor of Illinois [Len Small] that you will do so.

Very cordially yours,
Calvin Coolidge

The note was delivered by courier.[12]

President Coolidge and Congress did not think it appropriate that the federal government should be the primary source of disaster relief, nor did Coolidge think it appropriate for a standing president to tour the afflicted area. He was of the opinion any visit might be construed as political grandstanding. Coolidge believed it was the function of the independent states and charitable organizations to provide relief. This philosophical stance was sorely tested in 1927 when his beloved Vermont suffered a catastrophic flood. The capital city of Montpelier was inundated by forty feet of water from the rampaging Winooski River. The lieutenant governor of the state drowned in the floodwaters. In his state of the union address that year, the obdurate Coolidge failed to wobble. Instead, in as few words as possible he encapsulated the predicament by reiterating his stance: "The Government is not an insurer of its citizens against the hazard of the elements. . . . The Government does not undertake to reimburse its citizens for loss and damage incurred under such circumstances."[13]

Henry M. Baker, national director of Red Cross disaster relief, who by coincidence found himself in St. Louis for a previously scheduled regional meeting, was on his way on March 19 by Illinois Central coach to Carbondale, from which relief operations were to be orchestrated from a railroad warehouse next to the depot.

Among the unending list of responsibilities Baker shouldered was smooth coordination of the Red Cross and its herculean efforts to uplift the afflicted populace. The media instrument of immediate choice was the widespread usage of local newspaper. This typical announcement appeared in the extra edition of the March 23 *Murphysboro Daily Independent*: "Accommodations for 500 women and children in Pullman cars on tracks south of Illinois Central depot. See Red Cross Bureau at Elks' Club for permits. Meals will be served."

The goal of the Red Cross was to put razed communities back on their feet. A first task was to send a team of trained workers into the area to begin a comprehensive registration of families in need. This study was then used to determine losses, the value of family assets remaining, and the family's financial ability to rebuild. Very quickly a plan was crafted for each family. An award was agreed upon by committee with recommendations for replacement of furnishings, the reconstruction of a primary dwelling, food needs, clothing, and any other necessities of life that may be required.

Aid was clearly intended to help those whose insurance was not honored, those without casualty coverage, and those who simply could not afford the cost of providing shelter for their loved ones. Those who qualified could receive nonrecourse funds to rebuild their primary residences. Families who chose to rebuild a new home themselves were allotted $1,500 worth of materials from boxcars of building supplies. One DeSoto survivor owned a primary residence and twelve rental homes, all destroyed. The Red Cross refused to rebuild the rentals or did not replace business assets because it was not its mission to do so.

Controversy directed at the Red Cross in an Associated Press story from West Frankfort was addressed personally by Baker during a March 24 public meeting at the Murphysboro Presbyterian Church, the transcription of which was carried in its entirety on the front page of the Murphysboro *Daily Independent* the following morning. F. E. Burleson was the staff assistant to the Chapter Service Administration based in West Frankfort. During an earlier five-county meeting to discuss relief efforts, Burleson demanded to know the status of contributions received earmarked specifically for Egypt when the Red Cross withdrew its personnel. He insisted the funds stay in southern Illinois.

A hundred people listened to Baker's response as he set ground rules in an attempt to clearly outline what the Red Cross would and would not do. "Criticism, of course there will be criticism," he said. He made it clear his organization was all about "rehabilitation," explained that the Red Cross arrives immediately after a disaster and stays only as long as it is needed particularly when local organizations can handle the recovery effectively themselves, and that cash grants were unusual because the Red Cross preferred a requisition system in which the survivor directed the Red Cross to buy the goods or services from a particular merchant in the town in which relief was sought. "Perhaps the most important point," Baker said. "Is that relief is based on need. The policies of the Red Cross are self-explanatory. It is a chartered organization by Congress. The books are open at all times for inspection."[14] Baker was accorded a standing ovation. Despite the fact Burleson's question was answered in tangential fashion, the issue dropped from the public media.

Still working diligently, on March 29, seventy additional nurses were dispatched to Murphysboro from the Red Cross Reserve Nursing Corps in neighboring states. They were tasked with going house to house inquiring about the inhabitants and their state of health to ensure proper medical assistance. One survivor told of her and her sister hiding in an outdoor privy to avoid the nurses and their needles.[15]

The Missouri Pacific Railroad provided pro bono railcars. One went to DeSoto filled with furniture for those living in tents. Another carried roofing materials. A third contained a field hospital of twenty beds for McLeansboro in Hamilton County. Murphysboro received a commissary outfit of fifty men, two large tents for sleeping and dining, and a smaller kitchen tent. Pleas for additional furniture donations appeared in the *Carbondale Free Press* asking the distressed to call "Phone 103-K," the Red Cross household furnishings department located in the Christian Church.

Of course, farmers, too, were overwhelmed by the storm with damage to or complete loss of homes, barns, outbuildings, chicken coops, fences, and windmills used to pump water for livestock. An estimate from Springfield claimed 573 farms in the counties of Jackson, Franklin, Hamilton, and White were destroyed or damaged. Jackson County alone counted "92 farm houses destroyed, 89 barns, 91 outbuildings, 31 cows, 26 horses, and 696 chickens." By early April the Red Cross devised an ingenious plan. Multiple groups of fifty men were split into two cadres; one started walking the storm track in Petersburg, Indiana, where the storm dissipated, and the other in Gorham, Illinois. The teams helped farmers along the way with debris clearance from their fields so spring planting could begin on time.[16]

Generous contributions of money and goods came in from all over the country, some officially coordinated through the Red Cross but others were spontaneous like the mile-long convoy that motored over the Ohio River at Shawneetown to pass through Harrisburg with food, clothing, toiletries, and medical supplies collected in Kentucky and Indiana.

On March 24, the headline of Murphysboro *Daily Independent*'s lead story promised, "MURPHYSBORO TO RISE AGAIN LIKE LORRAINE." The article said, "Mayor George Huffman of Lorraine, Ohio, sent a letter to the Relief Committee in which he extolled the Red Cross' efforts to restore his town after a June 1924 tornado ripped through northern Ohio in which 78 people died, 451 were seriously injured, and 206 homes destroyed." "All of the towns that were wrecked by the recent tornado of March 18," Mayor Huffman asserted, "will come back just as Lorraine has done. The Red Cross will do for . . . Murphysboro exactly what it so nobly and thoroughly did for us." The uplifting letter assured the city the Red Cross will help with a "happy reconstruction," urged the city not to despair, and said that Murphysboro can look forward to "a return to prosperity in less than a year just as Lorraine has."

By December, most of the relief workers in Murphysboro were gone. They left after spending over $3 million ($39 million today) in donated funds to lift Egypt back on its feet.

Perhaps the most poignant of public remarks made by a person of influence was expressed by Levy, who was at first skeptical of the Red Cross assuming leadership in his town: "Frankly I was not much impressed [with them at first] because I thought [they] would probably furnish some bandages and maybe some hot coffee, and sandwiches. I realized my great mistake and soon became convinced that there is no organization in all the land rendering a greater service to humanity at a time of great need than the American Red Cross."[17]

OTHER RELIEF EFFORTS

In the more rural areas of the storm track, door-to-door sales of everything from soap to coffee to furniture were services the average housewife would have used to buy the necessities of life and a few extra indulgences when possible. Corporations like the Larkin Soap Company of Buffalo, New York, Avon Products, New York City, and Fuller Brush, Hartford, Connecticut would have been familiar names to most in the region Another distributor was Jewel Tea Company of Chicago, which donated six thousand pounds of coffee distributed throughout the region from Red Cross headquarters in Carbondale.

In Murphysboro, it was estimated, 20 percent of the households carried wind damage insurance, and most had fire coverage. Nevertheless, legal battles ensued between fire protection policyholders and the insurance companies when the insurance company lawyers maintained that the demise of the houses was from an uncovered event, namely, the wind, and that resultant fires were caused by that wind event; therefore, no claim was valid. Most families caught in this financial spider web lacked the means to pursue legal recourse and just gave up. However, help was on its way. Learning of the problems, in early April Governor Small sent three insurance inspectors to southern Illinois to investigate alleged insurance fraud: Rufus Kendall, chief examiner; Wendall E. Cable; and special examiner Thomas K. Sprague. The Franklin County Bar Association offered free legal services for homeowners fighting insurance companies. In addition, the governor sent veterinarians south to help care for livestock injured by the storm.[18]

NEWSPAPERS

Local newspapers were invaluable sources of news. Especially useful were the columns after columns of dead and injured so that families could find out what happened to loved ones. The papers were also loaded with tips on where to find immediate help. A quarter-page advertisement in the *Daily Independent* on Friday said, "Modern Woodman!—All Modern Woodman or Families of Modern Woodmen in Trouble See—Elmer Etherton, Clerk." No address was given. And "NOTICE!—Anyone having losses and insured with the Busch Agency apply at the Busch office. Adjusters in the office and we are paying claims.—H. J. Busch." And "Prudential Insurance Notice!—Claims: Now being paid. Call at the office. Addresses: Notify us of your temporary address. Disability: We pay for loss of one hand or foot or both hands, feet, or eyes as well as death."

And from the same paper in among the "Illustrated Adventures of Jack Dawes": "Policy Holders Metropolitan Insurance Company—If we can be of any assistance in any way, call at our office, Borger-Hardy Building, 1330 Walnut Street, Murphysboro. Death claims will be paid upon presentation by claimant." Next to that ad is in bold, block type, "PEP-ELIXO—FOR CONSTIPATION—THE GREAT EVIL THAT CAUSES SO MUCH MISCHIEF."

The day after the tornado, a *Daily Independent* ad read: "REWARD—Our Agent, Mr. H. S. Koonce, lost his life in the tornado near Twenty-First and Walnut when his car was wrecked. His collection book was lost. We will pay a reward of $5 for its return to E. H. Norman, Asst. Mgr, Metropolitan Life Company."

Public notices kept readers current: "Keep out of basements with open lights"; "Mobile & Ohio men register at once"; "Call for unclaimed telegrams"; and from the Murphysboro Relief Committee to prevent looting, "You must have a permit," which reminded residents that to enter what remained of their homes, they needed a permit.

Other notices include "Inspect flues before building a fire," "Do you want employment?" asked an employment bureau that had been opened in the Chamber of Commerce, "Phone A. G. Zelle for hearse service," "Be sure to boil all water," "Can you spare gowns and sheets for needy?" "Relief Committee needs underwear for children," and "Donations of canned goods needed." And this touching section, "A temporary home for children. Every person having orphans should report the matter at once to the Housing Committee at the Elks." Murphysboro was busy taking care of its own.

George W. Swafford advertised roofing for sale, two carloads, "prices the same as before the storm." "Don't Go Hungry! Serving Free Pan Cakes, Maple Syrup, and Coffee, Pillsbury Flour Mill Co," announced another ad. The plumbers who gathered to help rebuild Murphysboro agreed on a tough twenty-rule code of professional ethics as well as an hourly rate reduction from $1.25 an hour to $1. Similarly, in a quarter-page ad in the March 27 *Murphysboro Daily Independent*, nine Murphysboro "public-spirited merchants" "pledged NO Profiteering."

Despite the horror, despite seemingly insurmountable problems, Egypt and its strong and independent people went forward with no collective whines; rather, the region was grateful and said so. In the March 31, 1925,

Murphysboro Daily Independent was, "B. F. Parker, whose home at 503 North Sixteenth Street was destroyed, will be completely rebuilt. Although Mr. Parker is 74 years of age, he has not lost faith in his home town and its people," and in the same edition, "Toney Haney, Murphysboro, infant victim of the recent tornado, faces life today with a new hope. Surgeons at Chicago's St. Luke's Hospital have grafted new parts to the nose, lips, and chin of the boy in a plan to give him a whole new set of features. He was horribly mutilated. His mother is in a St. Louis hospital, her hip broken." The chances are highly likely not a single bill was presented to the Haney family.

In the March 21 *Benton Evening News*, a report said, "Gorham spurned all outside aid, although a food shortage threatened, until the Red Cross sent a carload of food. 'Gorham will fight its own battles,' said B. B. Easley, chief storekeeper of the town. 'There is a food shortage, but we can not let that get to the outside world.'"

Kindnesses too many to catalog passing from stranger to stranger, one American to another characterized the aftermath. Marie South Williams talked about the Red Cross and the organization's profound effect on DeSoto and how churches and individuals chipped in, too. Although not back to work for two weeks because she wanted to concentrate on her family, locate missing kin, and especially to tend to the burials of loved ones, Marie and her husband, Frank, collected goods of all kinds in their Carterville home, from canned produce to mounds of clothes to take to DeSoto. Chairs and whole bedsteads spilled out onto their porch. One day, Ms. Williams reported, DeSoto held thirty-seven funerals. In an era when women like Minnie Barnett sewed nearly all the clothes for their families, Ms. Williams recounted how the Seventh Day Adventists delivered enough new sewing machines to the flattened town that every mother who still lived could have a new one. She also told a touching tale about "some very rich fellow . . . from St. Louis" who came to DeSoto to clothe "dozens of families, [he] just outfitted them with new clothes. And he took them up to St. Louis. They'd never been to anything any bigger than DeSoto, you know." Many of the caskets for the DeSoto children were purchased by this same unnamed Good Samaritan.

▼

The tragedy shook the world, taking on international significance for a time, something quite rare for Egypt. Because of the mining towns' large populations of migrated workers from the marble-quarrying area around Carrera, Italy, King Victor Emmanuel of Italy and premier Benito Mussolini sent cables of condolence to the United States. Mussolini was in great pain at the time and in line for yet another stomach surgery to repair what was presumed to have been chronic ulcers. The US Embassy in Rome was "besieged by anxious crowds craving information while the telephones were busy all day."[19]

Pope Pius XI was deeply concerned about the welfare of his migrated flock living in the coalfields of southern Illinois. From Washington, D.C., Monsignor Fumasoni-Bioni, the Roman Catholic apostolic delegate, wired a telegram to Pius XI. Upon hearing the news, the pope's "eyes filled with tears [and he] was heard to pray to God that the disaster might not be as grave as the first indication. He ordered special prayers recited [at the Vatican] to invoke the mercy of God upon the stricken region."[20] Pius XI was known for his establishment of the doctrine of the rule of subsidiarity, a thesis that blended well with Coolidge's laissez-faire approach to disaster relief. The church doctrine echoed federalism in its contention that federal governments should defer to state and local governments to remedy local problems, that disaster remediation is not the federal government's purview.

Acting President Simons of Germany sent President Coolidge and the people of America a cable of sympathy. Kind messages were also received from Norway; Japan; Salvador; Sir Esme Howard, ambassador to the United States from Great Britain; and Carl Greve von Moltke, minister to the United States from Denmark.

The Tri-State Tornado inflicted damage so severe the area has never fully recovered. It goes without saying the tornado was hardly the sole reason, yet it may be argued this was the initial blow that began a long, downward economic spiral. For example, US Census figures for Jackson County, Illinois, for the period 1920 to 1930 show a decline in population of 3.8 percent. During the same term, population in Illinois increased by 16.9 percent and for the United States as a whole 16.2 percent. For Murphysboro, the census of 2010 shows a population of 7,970, a decline from when the tornado struck of 39 percent.[21]

Better roads, mass production of autos and trucks, and cheap gasoline doomed the railroads in America. The 1920s brought affordable mobility. In Murphysboro, Eileen Breeden Jones's father, Clarence, was an interurban engineer for the Murphysboro Electric Company and drove a regular trolley schedule to and from Carbondale. He lost his job when the line shut down in 1927, the same year State Route 13—the Logan Highway—became the hard road between Carbondale and Murphysboro.[22] A new bus company put the interurban out of business. Unable to find a job, the family of six left their hometown for a small farm north of DeSoto, owned by Eileen's maternal grandparents.[23]

As with Murphysboro, West Frankfort never again saw such widespread prosperity. Between 1910 and 1920, Franklin County's population grew an eye-popping 121 percent largely because of the lure of coal mining jobs. The next decade saw a modest increase of 3.8 percent, well behind the nation as a whole at 16.2 percent. West Frankfort's population since the Tri-State has fallen to 8,182 as reported in the census of 2010, a breathtaking decline of 54.5 percent. In comparison, between 1970 and 2010, the US population increased 241 percent. Income levels have also seriously lagged national statistical norms. National median family income (MFI) in 2010 was $64,400; in Murphysboro it was $34,987, or 54.3 percent of the average; and West Frankfort was about the same at $34,432, or 53.5 percent. Clearly, the towns have not fully participated in America's growth. When the mines closed, when the businesses left, so did prosperity.[24]

Conversely, Princeton, Indiana, continued to thrive. The H. J. Heinz Corporation and Southern Railway, the town's largest employers, rebuilt. Jobs stayed in Princeton, and its population in the years 1920–30 rose a robust 18.2 percent, two percentage points faster than the nation itself. The next decade contained the weary years of the Great Depression. Princeton grew by 10.2 percent, nearly 40 percent faster than the growth rate for the nation during the same time span. Gibson County's 2010 MFI is $44, 839, a healthy 70 percent of the national median in an area where the cost of living is considered very low when compared with more populated urban centers and suburbs, demographic areas that contain 82 percent of Americans. Clearly, the Pocket recovered. Egypt did not.[25]

One reason for this decline in southern Illinois is the Clean Air Act of 1990, an environmental regulatory nightmare for King Coal in southern Illinois. The act declared the region's abundant high-sulfur coal deposits too dirty to sell to the country's electric utilities. Coal generates half of America's daily consumption of electricity although that metric is falling due to a renewed war on coal usage. Mines closed in the Great Depression and then again in the ecopolitical firestorm of the 1990s. Coal production plummeted. Resultant chronic unemployment began to plague the citizenry. Unionization played a part as right-to-work states and overseas concerns wooed and won unionized manufacturing companies, such as Bunny Bread in Anna, World Color Press in Sparta, Brown Shoe in Murphysboro, and Norge-Whirlpool in Herrin, none of which is in the manufacturing business today in southern Illinois. Productivity gains created by technological improvements of mechanized coal-mining equipment displaced miners with pick axes who labored at the coal seam in 1925. The 1940s brought long-wall mining strategies that increased the number of machines underground proportionate to the decline in men needed to operate the efficient equipment. Another factor in the decline was that the nation began to rely more and more on petroleum and natural gas for home as well as industrial use. Coal-fired locomotives carried fewer and fewer passengers, and to make matters worse, by the early 1950s, diesel-powered locomotives replaced steam engines. The same phenomenon held true on the inland waterways as the first two decades of the twentieth century saw the coal-fired steamboat era die. In more contemporary times, an active Environmental Protection Agency has scuttled increased usage of coal for electricity generation by raising emissions mandates to levels that make coal's use both cost and legally prohibitive no matter what the sulfur content might be.

Recent years have seen globalization influence redevelopment of the high-sulfur coal so abundant in the region. The vast majority of increased production escapes restrictive US regulation on its way to China, shipped from the port of New Orleans much as the furs trapped in Egypt by the French, the British, Native Americans, and Americans did over three hundred years ago when Louis Quatorze, the Sun King of France, granted Sieur Charles Juchereau de St. Denis a charter to build a tannery near what is today Cairo, Illinois.

Although blessed with natural wealth, unlike central Illinois, Egypt does not have bottomless topsoils so agriculture could not contribute to a recovery sufficiently powerful to drive regional growth. The Illinoian glacier halted at an east-west line north of Carbondale. South of that city and along Route 13, the unglaciated Illinois Ozarks dominate the terrain, making the topography unsuited for large-scale row-cropping. In addition, Illinois Basin oil was never an economic boon in Jackson and Franklin Counties, the two counties that suffered the worst Tri-State Tornado damage. Ironically, both White and Hamilton Counties are situated in some of the most productive oil-bearing geology in the country, so population declines seen in the first decades of the twentieth century witnessed gradual replacement due to oil and gas services adding jobs that, in turn, regrew population counts.

During the many, many intriguing hours of research necessary to tell this astonishing story, Adlai Stevenson's remarks leaped to the forefront of all other rhetoric on the subject of the Tri-State Tornado when he spoke to the courage and tenacity with which southern Illinoisans attempted, albeit with only partial successful, to reload their lives: "To see on every side the human spirit triumphant over cruelty that has removed all that makes life worthwhile, is an exhibition of heroism and abiding faith in the essential rightness of things that surpasses all understanding. Indeed, the tornado disaster presents no greater moral lesson and no greater manifestation of magnificent stoicism than this steadfast endurance in the face of monumental adversity."[26]

It was also remarkable that neither one of the survivors interviewed—Betty Barnett Moroni and Eileen Breeden Jones—indicated even an inkling of political partisanship. No finger was pointed. No blame was heaped on any political party or relief agency nor did one town carp about a perceived differential in treatment. In the words of Ike Levy, the people of southern Illinois and the nation itself "gave generous and timely assistance [that] has given me new hope, much courage and great confidence in the future. The citizens of Murphysboro and vicinity feel deeply grateful and thankful for every assistance rendered them."[27] He asked that God bless his city's benefactors. Governor Small, whenever mentioned in print, never had a D or R after his name nor did any other elected state or federal official quoted in the papers of the day. This was not a political opportunity. The Tri-State Tornado was treated as the tragic disaster it was and whose remediation was for the benefit of those affected not aggrandizement of someone's public career.

The land laid waste by warring weather fronts happened to stripe a part of the nation defined by fierce individuality grown over the course of three

A solitary girl, her hands jammed into side pockets, inspecting the wreckage of a home in DeSoto, Illinois. Perhaps the pile of debris is the remnant of her own home or that of a deceased family member or schoolmate. Six army-issue tents stand in the background. *Photo courtesy of the West Franklin (Illinois) Historical District and Silkwood Inn Museum.*

hundred years by the determined frontier can-do attitudes of those French, British, Spanish, and, finally, Americans who pioneered southern Illinois. On that historic Wednesday in the middle of March 1925, southern Illinois suffered the most of the three states hit. Those left behind endured, learned to live without their lost loved ones, and got on with the business of life, as the widow Barnett did with her four children, a woman who braved the Great Depression as a single parent who refused aid by saying other people needed it. That same courageous narrative stretched from Annapolis to Gorham, and Murphysboro to DeSoto, and West Frankfort, Parrish, and Crossville to Griffin and Princeton.

However, through no fault of its sturdy people, life would never be the same in Egypt.

APPENDIX
NOTES
BIBLIOGRAPHY
INDEX

Appendix:
Rosters of the Dead by Town

This roster is not intended to be definitive and is included solely for reference. Where possible, the age of the victim is furnished.

GORHAM, ILLINOIS
From the *Murphysboro Daily Independent*, March 26, 1925

Murray Asbury
Charles Barton
Harve Bean
Sarah Bean
Margaret Brown
Bertha Casey
Martha Cole
June Crain (Crane), wife of C. Crain (Crane)
Ruben Crain (Crane) and his wife, Ollie
Delia (Della) Cross
Gerald Cross, 5 years old
Joe Robert Dunn
William Foncree
Lawrence Gale
Charles Gordon

Miss Sally Inchcliff
Dick Johnson
Andrew Moschenrose
Edward Moschenrose
Miss Louise "Lulu" Moschenrose
Mrs. Mary Moschenrose
Lafayette Needham
Mildred Marle Needham, infant
Gus Reeder
Nancy Reeder
Mrs. William Roeder
Opal Rosenberger
Frances Stamp
George Temure (sometimes Thormure)
Kitty White (sometimes Katy; cook at Wallace's Restaurant)

MURPHYSBORO, ILLINOIS
From the Jackson County Coroner's Report, April 1, 1925

John G. Andrews, 47
Clara Bailey, 55
Albert Baker
Emma Baker, 41
Mrs. Frank Baker
Millard Baker Jr., 14
Opal Baker, 4
Thelma Baker, 13, Longfellow School
G. S. Bandy, 80
Frank Baroli, 21
Joe Baroni, 3 months
Mary L. Batterush, 3 months
Eugene Beasley, 8
Minnie Beck, 25
Mrs. George Berger
Juanita Berger, 3
Margaret Berger, 28
John Berra, 65
E. J. Bjick, 30
Fredia Blacklock, 42
Bert Blackwood, 16
Jessie Bledso, 32
Evelyn Boston, 8, Logan School fatality
Dan Boucher (not D. L.), 64
Edna Imogene Boucher, 8
Martha L. Bowerman, 11, Logan School
Mrs. Mary Brandon, 75
John J. Brewer, 36
Alice Brown, 41, black
Joe Henry Brown, 3, black
Mrs. Lou Brown, 53, black
Freeman Bryan, 23
Angeline Buchholz, 32
John M. Cagdale, 93
Albert W. Callihan, 2
Jerry C. Callihan, 3
Elizabeth Carner
Howard Carr, Longfellow School
Earl Chrisler, 1
Kate Clemons, 18, black, Carbondale

William Cochran, 64
Willis Cochran
Ethel Rode Coffer, 12, Logan School
Constant Comte, 44
Helen Cook, 4
Joe Correnti's child
Mrs. Mary Correnti
Herbert Cristler—Fred Cristler's baby boy
Mrs. Mary C. Cupp
T. E. Darby, 27
Mary Ellen Davis, 13, Logan School
Grazia DeLuca (or Gratia), 3
DeLuca infant of Jake DeLuca
Marian DeLuca, 5
Joe DeWitt, 7
Henrietta Ditzler, 6, Longfellow School
Charles M. Dukes, 57
Arthur Dunn
Chapman Arthur Dunn, 24
Rounzey E. Eason, 8
David A. Ellis
C. F. Elmore, 50
Sylvester Ferguson, 25, Carbondale
Nellie Fielding, 32
Pauline Fielding, 3
Effie File, 30
Ella Flott, 38
Mary Etta Gibson, 54
James O. Gooch, 52, Salem, Tennessee
Y. G. Green, 30, black
Alworth A. Gregory, 29
Rose Margaret Griffin, 26
Louis Gualdoni, 26
Josephine Guy, 53
John Habermehl, 35
Ben Habermehl, 62
Barbara Ethel Hall, 29
Ruby Hall, 1
Della Hamlet, 24, black
Francis Abe Hammer, 1

Samuel Haney, 76
Ernest Hardwig, 64
John Gilford Harris, 68
L. C. Harrison, 12, Longfellow School
Ervin Hassebrock, 30
Junita Hayes, 7 months
Cudrey Heinny, 45, black
Jennie Alice Higgins, 64
Ernest Hinchcliff, 54
James Holliday, 5, black
Sarah C. Holliday, 64
Mary Edward Hopkins, 5, black
Mollie Hudgens, 26
Eliza Humphreys, 66
Will Hunziker, 38
Minnie Pearl Huppert, 32
Robert Icenogle, 12
Adolphy Isom, 75, black
Loney Jackson, 41
J. A. Janes, 75
Margaret Janes, 58, black
Sarah Janes, 64
Mrs. Jones, black
Mrs. Kelly, black
Francis Patrick Keough, 30
Sam Kerren, 39
Herbert T. (S.) Koonce, 42
Dorothy Launius, 18
Herbert Lennington, 33
Campbell Lipe, 40
Claude Lipe, 18
Evan Lipe, 74
Anna Bernice Loy, 28
Charles Edward Loy, 4 months
Thomas James Loy, 3
James Pete Martin, 8
John Martin, 5
Madeline Martin, 3 months
Mamie Martin, 35
Mary Maynor, 49
May Dell Martin, 2
Ben McAllister, 50, black
Oren McBride, 22

Victoria McBride, 64
Robert McCord, 6, Longfellow School
William E. McNeil Sr., 50
Jeremiah Newton Mifflin, 1
Louise H. Miller, 40
Louis E. Miller, 40
Joe Moore, 51
Essie Lee Nausley, 26
Zora Lee Nausley, 3
C. H. Nolte, 48
Herbert Addison Orland, 58
Della Pate, 23
Oscar Perkins, 53, black
Bertha May Pieron, 37
Mildred Pieron, 1 month
Lucile Piltz, 37
Robert Piltz, 1
Hugh Reeder, 36
Francis Riggo, 56
Paul Edward Roberts, 10, Logan School
Earl Russell, 18
Latisha Sampson, 82
Joe Schiro, 5
John Schiro Jr., 2
Josephine Schiro, 8
Laura Schiro, 30
Mildred Schiro, 4
Tessie Schmallenberger, 13, Logan
  School
Elizabeth Schoole, 22
Sadie Evelyn Shaw, 65
Bernard J. Sheley, 21, high school
Oliver Smith Silvey, 21
Rhoda Silvey, 64
Bertha F. Simons, 5, Longfellow School
Mrs. Slater, black
Ebbie Smith, 22
Ernest Smith, 22
Evelyn Marie Smith, 9
James Glannigan Smith, 58
John W. Spangler, 21
Josephine Spangler, 21
Dorris Stephenson, 5

Ruth Stephenson, 5
Bennie Stivers, 3
Elmer Stivers, 4
Cooper Stout, 51
A. F. Stratton, 4
Mrs. Sadie Stratton, 30, black
John Swafford, 54
Isabell This, 3
Louise This, 35
Louisa Thompson, 75
Octavia Trembly, 89
Annie Turner, 45
Henry Varner, 25

Herbert Varner, 4
Major Verbal, 8
Margaret Verbal, 78
Norman Varner, 2
William E. Varnum, 14, Longfellow
  School
John J. Wagner, 44
Emma Walker
Louis Roy Wayman, 8, Longfellow
  School
Mildred White, 13, Longfellow School
Frank Whittington, 35
Arah Will, 85

DESOTO

From the *Murphysboro Daily Independent*, March 26, 1925

Luther Austin
Ruby Austin
Bainbridge girl
Millard Baker
Elsie Barnett, 6, died Herrin Hospital
Marie Barnett, 9
Tina Mae Barnett, 12
Eugene Beasley
John Berra
George Boland, deputy sheriff
Mary L. Bolterbust
Leta Bourlaud
Ruby Bratcher
Ruth C. Bratcher, baby
Ethel Brown
Woodrow W. Brown
Walter Joseph Bullar
A. J. Caldwell
—— Dickson girl
Norman Dixon
Elna Espey
Thomas Ferrill
Viola Ford
Barbara Hall
Joseph Hartley
Everis Harvell

Georgia Harvell
Alva Heevlett
Elvain Hewlett
Harold Hughes
Fay(e) Hyde
R. L. Hyde
Hubert Iconogle
Man named Oliver ——
Francis Murray
Margaret J. Neal
Lucille A. Poulson
Rudolph Reed
Mr. and Mrs. Frank Redd
William Shankle
Francis Sills
Mrs. Clay Smith
Mrs. S. O. South
Emma E. Split
Son of Reverend Stecess
Lillian Ruth Taylor
Alonzo Temple
Helen Watts
Mrs. Westwood
Nora Will
Sarah Will
Frank Woods

HERRIN HOSPITAL

Thomas S. Adams
Mrs. Anna Beasons
Grady Clarence Beasons, child
Ida May Shirley
Claude Stonum, child

SCHROEDER'S FUNERAL HOME, DUQUOIN

Mrs. Henry Bullar
Mrs. Hugh
Rolla Hugh
Roberta Morrison
Miss Temple

WEINBERG'S FUNERAL HOME, DUQUOIN

Mrs. Nellie Bash
Mrs. Electra Noah Beasley
Richard Beasley
Mrs. Ida May Bratcher
Miss Ford
Musical Dan
Mrs. Sophia Schoen

WEST FRANKFORT

From the *West Frankfort Daily American*, April 4, 1925

Mrs. Sarah Aidlott
Margaret Arno
Bertha May Barnes
Earl Barnes
Mr. and Mrs. Baxanic
Raymond Bays
J. H. Bean
Mrs. Virgie Bell
Fred Biggs
Marguerite Biggs
Mrs. Biggs
John Black
George Boganie
Dushanka Bozewich
Billie Jean Brown
Frances AKA "Jessie" Brown
Jesse Brown
Jissut Brown
Wayne Brown
Budtka baby
Mrs. Fred Burbank
Gervia B. Burgess, 44, Johnston City, died January 2, 1926, of injuries
Chloe Emmett Burns

Ola Burton
Mrs. Joe Butler
Charles Campbell
Mrs. Charles Campbell
Edna Georgina Campbell—all her
  siblings died in the tornado;
  Edna was carried 400 feet in the
  tornado but survived; she died
  July 21, 1925, from typhoid fever
Jeanette Campbell
Joe Campbell
Ruth Campbell
Virgil Campbell
L. J. Carlton
Church child
Mrs. E. G. Clark
Connor child, subject of divorce
  custody battle between Ruby and
  Dwight Connor
Asa Cramer
Jeff Davis
Mrs. Jeff Davis
Charles Denton
Flora Dixon

Frank Donnor
Mrs. Minnie Donnor
G. W. Downing
John Drobish
Mary Estes
Mrs. Charles Fisher
Helen Footney, Belleville, Illinois
John Ford
Miss Loren Ford
Mrs. Nora Ford
Marion Gilbert
Walter Gilbert
Charles Gunter
Wesley Gunter Jr.
Mrs. Maggie Hammonds
Andrew Hancock
Loudean Hand
Mrs. Neil Hand
C. I. Hicks
Mrs. C. I. Hicks
Ruth Hicks, child
Harry Hill
Jacob Holland
Elizabeth Howard
Gertrude Hunter
Anna Lou Johnson, Plumfield, Illinois
Anna Karnes
daughter of Ike Karnes
daughter of Tim Karnes
Kenneth Karnes
Lorene Karnes, 5
Ordell Karnes
Oscar Karnes, 4
Randall Karnes
Roscoe Karnes, 6
Mrs. Tim Karnes
Vivian Karnes
Justine Kechroir
Nan Kelley
Stanley Lebach
Elmer Lester
Mary Lester

Elmer Lewis
Mrs. Stanley Lolovik
Mrs. Franzisk Manchura
J. A. Mason
James McGowan
Mrs. Frank McKoto
Frank McLellan
Cantrel Udel Munday
Morgan Munday
Bessie Neibel
Hattie Neibel
William Norris
—— Novotney
Mrs. John Oaks
Ida Ogdon
Malcom Ogdon
Nola Oller
Kenneth Oresley
Anna Ostroski
Ella Owsley
R. Owsley
Mrs. Amelia Ponovich, Belleville, Illinois
Steve Ponovich
child of Luther Pattillo
Wilma Pattillo
Joe Pleskovich
Steve Pleskovich
Homer Powell
Mrs. Violet Powell, Vienna, Illinois
Frank Pritchett, 25
Marshal Ramsey Jr.
Frank Razer
infant of C. P. Reed
Geraldine Remley
Gladys Rennley
infant of T. C. Ritings
T. C. Ritings
Mrs. Cora Roberts
Josie Roberts
Leroy Roberts
G. I. Russell
David Spencer Sanders, 60

Mrs. Jane Sanders, 56
Dollie Scott
Stella Scott
Anthony Shemansky
Mrs. Maggie Shopinsky
M. E. Silkwood
Mrs. Walter Smith
Andy Solcatch
Fred Sowerby
Elijah Stagner
Fred Stagner Jr.
Tommy Stagner
Clarence Sullivan
Ben Summers
Mrs. Fred Taylor
Geraldine Taylor
Stena Taylor
Harold Leigh Thomas
unidentified boy, 16
unidentified girl at Titsworth house

unidentified man, 32
unidentified man, 34
unidentified man, 35
unidentified man, 36
unidentified man, 38
unidentified man, 47
unidentified woman, 35
unidentified woman, 38
unidentified woman, 39
unidentified woman, 55
unidentified woman, 60
Bonnie Wampler, child
Mrs. Ralph Wampler
Joe Watson
Pearl Watson
Nora Edith Whittington
Elbert Williams, Ohio Valley
Mrs. James Williams
Tekla Ziskonski
Brown Zukoskia

PARRISH, ILLINOIS, AND VICINITY
From the *Benton Evening News*, March 21, 1925

Douglas Akin
James Biddle
Annie Gertrude Braden
Martha Braden
Robert Braden
Wilma Braden
Mrs. Joe Campbell, 52
Gertrude Clem, 54
James Clem, general store operator
Whit Conover
Billie Cunningham, 3
Hannah C. Cunningham
Andy Downs, 55
Mrs. Arlie Flanagan
Sam Flannigan
Lou Ella Galloway, 46
Royal Eugene Galloway, 14
John T. Gammons, 57
Mrs. Gray, 65

Mrs. Bert Gunter, 23
Charles Gunter
Christina Gunter, 3
Columbus Hicks and daughter-in-law
Mary Malinda Ing, 84
Bertha Kerley, 3
Mrs. Ettie Kerley, 47
Homer Kerley, 12
Otto Kerley, 12
Mrs. Isabelle Launius, 40
Mrs. Belle McFarland
Mr. Joe Melvin
Mrs. Joe Melvin
Beulah Price, 21
Jackie Jean Price, 1
Layman Price, 22
Lou Ella Price, baby
Raymond Price
Mrs. Debora Rainey, 52

William Rainey
Clella Shew
Hattie Smith
Ivan Smothers, 18 [reported in error]
Mrs. Silas Sullivan
Kenneth Taylor, 3
Merl Taylor, 4

Unidentified female, white
Unidentified male, black, possibly the man reported riding a mule spooked by a passing car and thrown into its windshield
Unidentified male, white
Ivory Williams, 32

HAMILTON COUNTY, ILLINOIS
From the *Carmi (IL) Times-Tribune*, March 28, 1925

MACEDONIA
John Lampley, 65

MCLEANSBORO AREA
Mrs. Martha Adams, 74, Route 7
Robert P. Adams, 74, Route 7
Mrs. Edna Shelton Ballard, 23, Route 6
Lottie (Lotta) Jane Ballard, 1, Route 6
Mrs. Mary (Edna) Ballard, 52, Route 6
Vonna May Ballard, Route 6
Letha McElyea Brockett
Margarete Cantrell, widow
Charles Chalon, Crook Township
W. Charles Cheek, 45
Mrs. Janie Cheek, 48, Route 6
Wesley Cluck, 40, Route 5
Edna Fern
Ollie Flannigan, 40, Route 4
Sam Flannigan, 38, Route 4
Mrs. Media Forester, 25, St. Louis, pregnant
Mrs. Rosetta Webb Hicks
Mrs. Rosetta Hollister, 49, Route 7
W. Sumner Hollister, 49, Route7, drowned in Lick Creek

Carl Hunt, 21, Route 4
John B. Lockwood, 71, Route 3
Emery Loyd, 44, Route 6
Earl Mayberry, 12, Route 5
Thomas McMurtry
Nellie Mick, Mayberry Township
Mrs. Walter Mick, Route 5
Frank M. Oglesby, 60, Route 3
Rella Oglesby, 37
Reverend Francis Pittman, 50, Route 4
Charles Leslie Prince, 1, Route 7
Mrs. Minerva Ray, 44, Route 7
John Raymond, Crook Township
Edna Shelton
Belva Smith, 17, Route 3
Lonnie Smith, 45, Route 3
Mrs. Lillie Lockwood Smith, 40, Route 3
Roy Smith, 21, Route 3
Mina Gertrude Taylor, 8, Route 6
John Raymond Van Winkle, 26, Route 7
Mrs. Charles America Webb, Route 7

THOMPSONVILLE
Martha Hicks, 48, Flannigan Township

WHITE COUNTY, ILLINOIS

From Bob Johns, *The 1925 Tri-State Tornado's Devastation in Franklin County, Hamilton County, and White County, Illinois*

Charles Argo, visiting Worthen's
Snowden Biggerstaff, teacher
Herman Bingham, 13, Hadden School
Helen Clark
William Dietz
Wilburn Felty, 9, Frieberger School
Vernon Miller, 12, at Trousdale School
Jasper Mossberger
Arminite Murdach
Lucy Ellen Phillips, James Boland's sister
Alvin Rhein

Ethel Murdach Rhein (Mrs. Alvin)
William Richardson, carpenter, Eldorado
Rosa A. Smith, James Boland's mother
George Speck
Baby Warthen
Delbert Warthen
Harold Edward Warthen
Versa Warthen, 4
John "Strawberry" Wilson
Lottie Winter (Mrs. John)

CROSSVILLE, ILLINOIS, AND VICINITY

From various sources

Fred Bennett, 22
Fairzine Fitzgerald
Harvey Jordan and small daughter
Three Jones sisters

Barbara Mauer
Elma Stokes
John Winter

GRIFFIN, INDIANA

From a memorial erected by the Village of Griffin, First and Main Streets, Griffin Memorial Park, dedicated January 1, 2004

C. Allen
S. R. Biggerstaff, 35
Ethel Carr
Ruby Cleveland, 14
Clarence Combs
Clarence Corby
Mary Cox
Irene Daugherty
Elizabeth Denby
Elsie Elsperman
Mrs. Charles Elsterman
Winifred Fisher
William Gregory
——— Hanshoe
Helen Harris

Virgil Horton
Nina House, 34
Sidney Hyatt, 35
Wilmer Kern
Mrs. Flo Kokomoor
Mary L. Kokomoor
James Lamar
Charles Majors
Ida Majors
M. Thomas Nottingham
James Oldham
Roy "Chick" Oller
Lester Price
Mrs. William Price
William T. Price Jr.

Auburn Saunders
Claude Schnarr
Virgil Simmons
Charles Stallings
Ida Stallings
Harry A. Stoneberger
T. Wade Stratton Jr., 14
Albert Strickland
Bessie Strickland
Miranda Thomas

Harry Vanway
Helen Vanway
William J. Westheiderman
Golden Williams, 40,
  identified by clothing
  and boots
E. S. Woods
William A. Woods
Clarisse Young, 14
Vera Young

OWENSVILLE, INDIANA

From the *Kokomo (IN) Daily Tribune*, March 19, 1925

Lucy King
Mrs. Walter King
Walter King
William King

Lemuel Waters and small son
Mrs. Lemuel Waters
Richard Waters, 70
Mr. and Mrs. Elvis Williams

PRINCETON, INDIANA

From the *Davenport (IA) Democrat and Leader* and the *Kokomo (IN) Daily Tribune*, March 19, 1925

Robert Brammer, 70
Marietha Brokaw, 10
Miss Nellie Cooper, 17
Mrs. Harvey Jordan and small
  daughter
Sam Key and his two children
Ada McClurkin
Mrs. Archie McClurkin
Mrs. Harriet McClurkin
Miss Hazel McGarrah, 16
Mrs. Frank Metzger, 42

Mrs. Mary Miller
Mrs. Thomas Nash, 50
Viola Nuthman, 10
Mrs. Clyde Osborne, 32
Ora Perry, 40
Aubrey Rankin, 35, (East St. Louis)
Riley Reeves, 35
James Wallace
James Whitten, 4
Edna Wilkinson, 12
George Wilkinson, 10

ELIZABETH, INDIANA

From the *Davenport (IA) Democrat and Leader* and the *Kokomo (IN) Daily Tribune*, March 19, 1925

Mrs. Mattie Hoke
Vivian Hoke

Mrs. Charles Rhodes

Notes

1. GENESIS, 1 P.M.: ANNAPOLIS, MISSOURI, TO GORHAM, ILLINOIS

1. *Murphysboro (IL) Daily Republican*, March 21, 1925, 2.

2. *Benton (IL) Evening News*, March 21, 1925. J. P. Glen, the only record keeper in Gorham, openly admitted the death totals could be wrong, which explains the wide variances seen in the literature of the official number of Gorham dead.

3. *St. Louis Post-Dispatch*, March 20, 1925, 2.

4. Ibid.

5. Joy, "Great Tornado," 9.

6. Salzmann, *Murphysboro Tornado*, 72B–72G.

2. MURPHYSBORO, ILLINOIS

1. *Murphysboro (IL) Daily Independent*, golden anniversary of publication ed., October 16, 1923.

2. Allen, *It Happened*, 111–12.

3. A *chivari* (also shivaree, callythumping, bull-banding) derives from a medieval French tradition called *charivari* and is thought to be a holdover from when the French culture dominated the Mississippi Valley in the first half of the eighteenth century. Usually begun after the newlyweds have gone to bed, a chivari is a rude, noisy ruckus generated from anything that can make an obnoxious racket from washtubs being beaten to horns, bells, and the like. After a time, the door to the assaulted house is expected to be opened and refreshments served, or as was the case in Murphysboro even though this was the heart of Prohibition, the bridegroom takes the men to the nearest tavern.

The ladies were on their own. At times a chivari can also assume a negative function and perhaps this is the case with the new Mr. and Mrs. Gualdoni. Perhaps their friends or family disapproved. One can only speculate. Allen, *Legends and Lore*, 82–83.

4. *St. Louis Post-Dispatch*, March 21, 1925, 4. In the hours and hours of research for this narrative, the author could find not another word about Buster Brown. A three-year-old John Henry Brown, a black toddler, died, but he was the only male Brown on the Murphysboro roster (see appendix).

5. Eileen Breeden Jones, interview with author, August 8, 2011, DeSoto, Illinois.

6. *St. Louis Post-Dispatch*, March 21, 1925, 2.

7. Felknor, *Tri-State Tornado*, 58. The Stecher Brewing Company operated under various names from 1867 to 1940. The site was razed in 1980.

8. Smith, *History*, 1053.

9. Kimmel, "Personal Account."

10. Ibid.

11. *Murphysboro (IL) Daily Independent*, March 21, 1925, 1.

12. *St. Louis Post-Dispatch*, March 20, 1925, 4.

13. Ibid.

14. *Murphysboro (IL) Daily Independent*, March 22, 1925.

15. *Benton (IL) Evening News*, March 23, 1925.

16. Sam O'Neil, *St. Louis Post-Dispatch*, March 22, 1925, 2.

17. *Benton (IL) Evening News*, March 23, 1925.

18. Frost, *Voices from Murphysboro*.

19. Joseph A. Melvin, research paper, n.d., file "Tornado 1925," archives, Jackson County Historical Society.

20. Ibid.

21. Colonel S. O. Tripp to Levy, memorandum, in Salzmann, *Murphysboro Tornado*.

22. Ibid.

23. *Resort* is an archaic term for a house of entertainment. The Murphysboro address may have served as a black-only bar/restaurant, or a gambling parlor, or a bawdy house, or some combination. In 1925 Murphysboro was one of the few towns in southern Illinois in which whites and blacks lived in the same community, yet blacks were rigorously segregated. They lived in a specific part of town, patronized black-run businesses, worshiped in their own churches, and were educated in separate schools.

24. *St. Louis Globe Democrat*, March 20, 1925; *Murphysboro (IL) Daily Republican*, March 27, 1925; *West Frankfort (IL) Daily American*, special ed., April 4, 1925.

25. *Murphysboro (IL) Daily Republican*, March 27, 1925.

26. Jones, interview.

27. *Murphysboro (IL) Daily Republican*, March 27, 1925.

28. Joy, "Great Tornado," 4.

29. *Pantagraph*, Bloomington-Normal, Illinois, March 20, 1925, 1.

30. Ibid., 32.

31. Joy, "Great Tornado," 6.

32. Ibid.

33. Joy, "Great Tornado," 24.

34. *Murphysboro (IL) Daily Independent*, March 21, 1925, 5.

35. Sam O'Neil, *St. Louis Post-Dispatch*, March 22, 1925, 2.

36. Henry M. Baker to Isaac Levy, in Salzmann, *Murphysboro Tornado*, 98A.

3. DESOTO, ILLINOIS

1. Henry M. Baker to Isaac Levy, in Salzmann, *Murphysboro Tornado*, 98A.

2. *Carbondale (IL) Free Press*, March 26, 1925, 2.

3. Illinois Coal Industry, *Report*, 7.

4. Dewmaine, Illinois, was an unincorporated, racially segregated mining camp thirteen miles east from DeSoto and built around a coal mine on the north edge of Carterville.

5. Williams, interview, 37–38.

6. Felknor, *Tri-State Tornado*, 33.

7. Ibid.

8. Betty Barnett Moroni, interview with author, June 2011, DeSoto, Illinois. Mrs. Moroni graciously gave the interview.

9. Williams, interview, 171.

10. *St. Louis Post-Dispatch*, March 20, 1925, 7.

11. Felknor, *Tri-State Tornado*, 33.

12. Moroni, interview.

13. Felknor, *Tri-State Tornado*, 42.

14. *New York Times*, March 19, 1925, 2.

15. *Mt. Vernon (IL) Register-News*, March 19, 1925.

16. Felknor, *Tri-State Tornado*, 33.

17. Williams, interview, 174.

18. Ibid., 176.

19. *New York Times*, March 21, 1925, 2.

20. *Mt. Vernon (IL) Register-News*, March 19, 1925.

21. Ibid.

22. Felknor, *Tri-State Tornado*, 33.

23. *Chicago Tribune*, March 21, 1925.

24. *Carbondale (IL) Free Press*, March 20, 1925, 4.

25. Ibid.

26. State Route 2 would become US Route 51 a year later, in 1926.

27. *St. Louis Post-Dispatch*, March 22, 1925, 5.

28. Moroni, interview.

29. *St. Louis Post-Dispatch*, March 21, 1925, 5.

30. *Carbondale (IL) Free Press*, March 21, 1925, 4.

4. WEST FRANKFORT, ILLINOIS

1. *West Frankfort (IL) Daily American*, April 3, 1925.

2. *Alton (IL) Evening Telegraph*, March 20, 1924.

3. Johns, *1925 Tri-State Tornado's Devastation*.

4. Carrier, *Little Bit of Heaven*, 109.

5. *New York Times*, March 19, 1925, 2.

6. *West Frankfort (IL) Daily American*, April 4, 1925, spec. ed.

7. *Benton (IL) Evening News*, March 19, 1925.

8. *St. Louis Globe-Democrat*, March 19, 1925.

9. *West Frankfort (IL) Daily American*, April 4, 1925, spec. ed.

10. *Benton (IL) Evening News*, March 20, 1925. Fatigue and disorientation are diagnostic symptoms of a concussion, from which Mr. Williams probably suffered.

11. *West Frankfort (IL) Daily American*, March 20, 1925.

12. Johns, *1925 Tri-State Tornado's Devastation*, 33.

13. *West Frankfort (IL) Daily American*, April 3, 1925.

14. *St. Louis Post-Dispatch*, March 21, 1925.

5. PARRISH AND CROSSVILLE, ILLINOIS; GRIFFIN, OWENSVILLE, AND PRINCETON, INDIANA; DISSIPATION

1. Akin, *Forgotten Storm*, 99.

2. *St. Louis Post-Dispatch*, March 20, 1925, 2.

3. Johns, *1925 Tri-State Tornado's Devastation*, 43.

4. *St. Louis Post-Dispatch*, March 20, 1925, 2.

5. Johns, *1925 Tri-State Tornado's Devastation*, 45.

6. Akin, *Forgotten Storm*, 106.

7. Johns, *1925 Tri-State Tornado's Devastation*, 66.

8. Ibid., 102.

9. Nipper, "Tornado."

10. *Carmi (IL) Times*, March 19, 1925, 1.

11. Thiem, *Prairie Farmer*.

12. *Carmi (IL) Times-Tribune*, March 20, 1925, 1.

13. Ibid.; ibid., December 9, 1965, 1.

14. Arthur H. Schneff, *St. Louis Post-Dispatch*, March 20, 1925, 1.

15. *St. Louis Post-Dispatch*, March 21, 1925, 1.

16. Johns, *1925 Tri-State Tornado's Devastation*, 129.

17. Ibid., 143.

18. Akin, *Forgotten Storm*, 113.

19. Felknor, *Tri-State Tornado*, 47.

20. Akin, *Forgotten Storm*, 62–64.

21. Johns, *1925 Tri-State Tornado's Devastation*.

22. Felknor, *Tri-State Tornado*, 58.

23. *Princeton (IN) Clarion*, March 19, 1925, 1.

24. Felknor, *Tri-State Tornado*, 30.

25. Mildred Field, diary, March 29, 1925, in Shaffer, "Tri-State Tornado, 7–8; *Princeton (IN) Clarion*, March 19, 1925, 1.

26. Akin, *Forgotten Storm*, 119.

6. AFTERMATH

1. Henry M. Baker to Isaac Levy, June 15, 1925, in Salzmann, *Murphysboro Tornado*, 72B–72.

2. Akin, *Forgotten Storm*, 94–97.

3. *Logansport (IN) Morning Press*, March 20, 1925, 1.

4. *St. Louis Post-Dispatch*, March 21, 1925.

5. Rhoads, "Hall of Fame."

6. *New York Times*, March 20, 1925.

7. Russell, *Southern Illinois Album*, xxvii.

8. Dan Lichtenstein to Isaac Levy, in Salzmann, *Murphysboro Tornado*.

9. *History of West Frankfort*.

10. H. N. Cupp, Jackson County Superintendent of Schools, to Isaac Levy, in Salzmann, *Murphysboro Tornado*, 46-B.

11. Relief Committee correspondence, in Salzmann, *Murphysboro Tornado*, 3.

12. "Coolidge Speaks, Red Cross Relief," *New York Times*, March 20, 1925, 1.

13. Coolidge, "State of the Union Addresses."

14. *Carbondale (IL) Free Press*, March 27, 1925.

15. Carrier, *Little Bit of Heaven*.

16. Joy, "Great Tornado," 24–25.

17. Isaac Levy, note, in Salzmann, *Murphysboro Tornado*, 1:3. Levy would serve his community as state's attorney, school board member, president of the Jackson County and various state bar associations, president of the Chamber of Commerce, and many other civic and charitable organizations. When his city needed him, Levy rose to the occasion.

18. *Benton (IL) Evening News*, March 28, 1925.

19. *New York Times*, March 21, 1925, 2.

20. Ibid.

21. "Murphysboro, Illinois"; US National Archives, "Census Records."

22. Jones, interview. The hard road is named in honor of Murphysboro-born Brigadier General John A. (Blackjack) Logan, a close contemporary of Generals

Ulysses Grant and William Tecumseh Sherman. Logan commanded in the Western theater of the Civil War. In 1884, he was the Republican vice presidential nomination on James Blaine's losing ticket.

23. *Pantagraph* (Bloomington, IL), March 23, 1925, 1.

24. "West Frankfort"; "Murphysboro, Illinois"; US National Archives, "Census Records."

25. US National Archives, "Census Records."

26. *Pantagraph* (Bloomington, IL), March 23, 1925, 1.

27. Isaac Levy, "To the Public," n.d., copy of TS, no file number, in Salzmann, *Murphysboro Tornado*.

Bibliography

Akin, Wallace. *The Forgotten Storm: The Great Tri-State Tornado of 1925*. Guilford, CT: Lyons, 2002.

Allen, John. *It Happened in Southern Illinois*. Carbondale: Southern Illinois University Press, 1968.

———. *Legends and Lore*. Carbondale: Southern Illinois University Graphics, 1963.

Angle, Paul M. *Bloody Williamson: A Chapter in American Lawlessness*. New York: Knopf, 1981.

Brush, Daniel. *Growing Up in Southern Illinois*. Chicago: Lakeside, 1944.

Carrier, James T. *A Little Bit of Heaven and a Whole Lot of Hell*. Greenfield, IN: EULA, 1998.

Coal Miner's Handbook, The. Scranton, PA: International, 1913.

Coolidge, Calvin. "State of the Union Addresses: Calvin Coolidge, December 6, 1927." *infoplease*. http://www.infoplease.com/t/hist/state-of-the-union/139.html.

Felknor, Peter S. *The Tri-State Tornado: The Story of America's Greatest Tornado Disaster*. Ames: Iowa State University Press, 1992.

Frost, Vickie, ed. *Voices from Murphysboro*. Murphysboro, IL: Murphysboro Pride Group, 1993.

Hale, Stanley J., ed. *The Williamson County (IL) Sesquicentennial Celebration Edition*. Marion, IL: Williamson County History Book Committee, 1993.

Hall, Andy. "The Ku Klux Klan in Southern Illinois in 1875." *Journal of the State of Illinois Historical Society* 46, no. 4 (1953): 27–34.

Hamilton County Historical Society of Illinois, McLeansboro.

Hartley, Harold Ray. *Way Down in Egyptland*. Oklahoma City, OK: Maverick, 1982.

History of West Frankfort, Illinois. Danville, IL: Frankfort Area Historical Society, 1978.

Illinois Coal Industry, The. *Report of the Office of Coal Development.* Springfield: State of Illinois, June 2008.

International Correspondence Schools. *The Coal Miner's Handbook: A Handy Reference Book for Coal Miners, Pit Bosses, Farmers Superintendents, Managers, Engineers, and All Persons Interested in the Subject of Coal Mining.* Scranton, PA: International, 1926.

Jackson County Historical Society of Illinois, Murphysboro.

Johns, Bob. *The 1925 Tri-State Tornado's Devastation in Franklin County, Hamilton County, and White County, Illinois.* Bloomington, IN: AuthorHouse, 2012.

Joy, Judith. "The Great Tornado of 1925." *Illinois—The Magazine of Illinois,* March 1978, 8–30.

Kimmel, Wilma Theiss. "A Personal Account of the 1925 Tornado and Its Effect on the Theiss/Hartmann Family of Murphysboro—a Recollection of a Monumental Disaster 67 Years Later." Contributed by Carol Allsup. *Jackson County IL GenWeb,* June 1992. http://jackson.pikecoilgenweb.org/1925tornado.html.

"Murphysboro, Illinois." *Wikipedia.* http://en.wikipedia.org/wiki/Murphysboro,_Illinois.

"1925 Tri-State Tornado: County Infirmary Is a Splendid Hospital." March 19, 1925. *Genealogy Trails,* 2014. genealogytrails.com/ill/white/il_white_tornado.htm.

Nipper, Geneva. "The Tornado of March 18, 1925." *McLeansboro.com,* March 10, 2001. http://www.mcleansboro.net/history/tornado_of_1925.php.

Palmer, Virgil O. *Come Walk with Me.* Utica, KY: McDowell, 1987.

Rhoads, Mark. "Hall of Fame: Lindbergh in Illinois." June 20, 2006. *Illinois Review.* http://illinoisreview.typepad.com/illinoisreview/2006/06/hall_of_fame_li.html.

Russell, Herbert K. *A Southern Illinois Album.* Carbondale: Southern Illinois University Press, 1990.

Salzmann, Katharine, ed. *Murphysboro Tornado, March 18, 1925: Relief Correspondence.* 3 vols. Murphysboro, IL: Sallie Logan Public Library, 2003.

Shaffer, Kelly. "Tri-State Tornado." Master's thesis, University of Southern Indiana.

Smith, George Washington. *The History of Southern Illinois.* Chicago: Lewis, 1912.

Thiem, E. G. *Prairie Farmer,* 97, no. 13, March 28, 1925.

US National Archives and Records Administration. "Census Records." http://www.archives.gov/research/census/.

"West Frankfort." Wikipedia. http://en.wikipedia.org/wiki/West_Frankfort, _Illinois.

West Franklin Historical District and Silkwood Inn Museum of Illinois, Mulkeytown.

White County Historical Society of Illinois, Carmi.

Williams, Marie South. Interview by Elizabeth K. Dixon. November 5, 1984, Springfield, Illinois. *Marie South Williams Memoir.* Archives/Special Collections LIB 144, Norris L. Brookens Library, University of Illinois at Springfield. www.uis.edu/archives/memoirs/WILLIAMSMvI.pdf.

Wilson, John W., and Stanley A. Changnon Jr. *Illinois Tornadoes.* Circular 103. Urbana: Illinois State Water Survey, 1971. http://isws.illinois.edu/pubdoc/C/ISWSC-103.pdf.

Index

Page numbers in italics denote images.

National Guard, 26, 29–30, 59, 98, 101; 139th Field Artillery, Battery E, 85–86
National Guard Armory, 28
National Weather Bureau, 93
Native Americans, 6
Neal School (West Frankfort, IL), 71
New Addition (West Frankfort, IL), 62–65, *63, 65, 70*
New Harmony, Indiana, 86
New Orient No. 2 coal mine, 62, 62–64, *72*
newspapers, 94–96, 105–7
New York City Police Band, 99
New York Times, 96
New York World, 97
Nipper, Geneva, 80
Nipper, June, 80
Norman, Charles, 30
North American Aerospace Command (NORAD), 93

Odd Fellows, 46
Old Ben No. 8 coal mine, 62, 92
Olga School, 77
108th Medical Regiment, 34
130th US Infantry Regiment, 3rd Battalion, 29–30
O'Neil, Frank, 82
O'Neil, Samuel, 25, 46, 51
Owens, Percy, 28
Owensville, Indiana, 86–87

Paegelow (colonel), 57
Panama Canal, 13
Pankey, Jesse, 56
Pantagraph (Bloomington, IL), 33
Parke-Davis Company, 94
Parker, B. F., 107
Parker Prairie School, 77
Parks, Margaret, 75
Parks family, *75*

Parrish, Illinois, 73–76, 91
Parrish School, 74
Peabody Coal Company, 70
Peabody Mine No. 18, 70–71, *71*
Pennington, J. J., 75
Perryman, Delmar, 74
Phillips Township, 83
Pius XI, 108
plumbers, 106
Pocket (Indiana), 84, 109
political partisanship, 111
Poplar Ridge School, 83
Porter, Eugene, 19
Prairie Farmer, 82
Princeton, Indiana, 86, 87–89, 109
Prohibition, 19, 28

radar, 93
radio, telephone, and film technology, 96–98
railroads, 12, 15–16, 98, 108; mercy missions, 25, 33, 75, 86, 103–4
railroad towns, 24, 87
Rathert, Elsie, 26–27
Rawlinson, Edna Ethel, 83
Rawlinson, Howard, 82
Red Cross, 57, 59, 77, 82, 97, 98–99, 101–5
Red Cross Disaster Relief (Carbondale, IL), 93–94
Red Cross Reserve Nursing Corps, 102
Redd, Frank, *43, 46*
Reed, Becky, 64
regiments: 108th Medical, 34; 130th US Infantry, 3rd Battalion, 29–30
Rein, J. E., 28
Reliance Milling Company, 13, *14*, 23
relief effort, 38, 40–41, 74–75, 82, 90; airplanes, 93–96; government involvement, 98–100; other efforts, 105; railroad mercy missions, 25, 33, 75, 86, 103–4; Red Cross, 101–5

GEOFF PARTLOW is a freelance writer of both fiction and nonfiction. A resident of southern Illinois for over forty years, he knows the history and the region's people and is uniquely qualified to bring sensitivity to the telling of the story of Egypt's historic disaster, the Tri-State Tornado. Geoff lives with his wife, Sarah, in Hilton Head, South Carolina.

 *A Shawnee Book*